Technology, Business, Human Resources, and Education

Public Speeches of:

Michael Stephen Bird, Ph.D.

This is a collection of public speeches given by Dr. Michael Stephen Bird over the past decade covering many topics. In these talks, he has presented his thoughts of technology, business, human resources, education, and religion. He is currently an educator, author, and public speaker.

Table of Contents

Disclaimer and History of Michael Stephen Bird, Ph.D.

Disclaimer: This book contains speeches of Dr. Michael Stephen Bird covering various topics such as technology, business, human resources, and education. His speeches and the contents in this book represent his thoughts, opinions, and research. The content of these speeches do not necessary reflect the opinion of any group, company, institution, or university that he may be affiliated with now or in the past. His presentations printed in this publication are independent of those organizations.

History: Dr. Michael Stephen Bird was born to Rev. John S. Bird and Ellen Bays Bird in Clarksburg, West Virginia on May 4, 1960. After moving to Florida, Dr. Bird went to high school at Bayshore High School and graduated in 1978. When Dr. Bird was sixteen years old, his father died due to complications in an open heart surgery. At this time, Dr. Bird started his first job at a local grocery store in Bradenton where he eventually worked around forty hours a week unloading trucks and stocking shelves. He was selected to be in the management training program even while he was still in high school and learned grocery merchandising, frozen food management, and produce management.

In 1978, he enrolled in Manatee Community College and worked at Manatee Federal Savings and Loan. In 1980, Dr. Bird went on to study Accounting at University of South Florida and graduated in 1981. His first professional job was a Bank Financial Auditor at First Federal of Broward which later became Glendale Federal Savings Bank. Within a year of his four year tenure at the bank, he moved on to work as an Internal Control Specialist and Internal Fraud Investigator. He passed the CPA exam in 1985 but never became a CPA because he lost interest in the Accounting field. After leaving Glendale Federal, he started to sell insurance and annuity plans by going door to door for six months. Following his short sales career, he worked as an Internal Control Specialist and an Information Systems Auditor at Florida Federal Savings and Loan. He obtained his Certified Internal Auditor (CIA) and Certified Information Systems Auditor (CISA) while working at Florida Federal.

On April 11, 1988, Dr. Bird moved to an area that later became Doral, Florida. He started his seventeen-year career at Carnival Cruise Lines. At the cruise line, Dr. Bird was an IT Auditor,  IT and Voice Systems Disaster Recovery Coordinator, Systems Security Manager, Application Software Developer, IT Quality Control Analyst, Quality Assurance Supervisor, IT Software Project Manager, and IT Configuration Management. There were times where Michael worked two positions at Carnival at the same time, where he developed the talent of multi-tasking.

Some key projects at Carnival included a comprehensive disaster recovery plan (1990), office services mailroom system (1991), front end system security system for the mainframe (1992), automated mass compile system (1994), Y2K Project - Mainframe, MAPPER Systems, and Vendor Management (1999), automated configuration management system for legacy application (2002), and worked many other projects in various platforms (legacy and non-legacy applications). He retired early from Carnival Cruise Lines and in 2005 he became a professional educator, author, and professional speaker.

He earned his Master's Degree in Business Administration from Nova Southeastern University in 1998 and his doctorate (PhD) from Capella University in Organizational Management with a specialization in Information Technology in 2010. His teaching career began in February 2004 as an adjunct professor and then moved into a full time professor position in February 2005. His dissertation is published and is called, "UTILIZING AGILE SOFTWARE DEVELOPMENT AS AN EFFECTIVE AND EFFICIENT PROCESS TO REDUCE DEVELOPMENT TIME AND MAINTAIN QUALITY SOFTWARE DELIVERY."

Dr. Bird has written "Chapter 12" in a book published in India entitled, "Managing Software Professionals." He has written many published online articles about education, technology, project management, and managing diversity. He has also published books that are available at Amazon.com, Barnes and

Noble, and other online bookstores. Dr. Bird also has done some public speaking from time to time on various topics such as Agile Software Development, Time Management, Edutaining to Create Interest in the Classroom, Software Project Management, and much more.

Dr. Bird married his wife, Rose-Lynn Cavaretta, in 1990 and they both raised three children in South Florida. He considers his wife as an important factor to his success as a professional educator, public speaker, and author. Dr. Bird's hobbies include performing comedy, watching movies, and going to activities with his wife. He attends church with his wife and they are practicing Christians. As a comedian, Dr. Bird has performed many performances at various clubs under a different stage name and also produced four actual comedy shows in both Broward and Palm Beach Counties. Dr. Bird's comedy hobby career started in middle school when he performed Mr. Thumbs in a religious musical called, Natural High. He provided the comic relief for what was generally a serious play. His legs were used in a beach scene for the movie, Where the Boys Are 84. In this movie, he was part of the extras walking behind the two stars on Ft. Lauderdale Beach. Dr. Bird loves to perform in front of audience. He is a natural at public speaking events as he engages his audience.

This book is a collection of some recent speaking events that Dr. Bird has delivered to a variety of audiences.

Business and Technology

Speeches related to business and technologies are presented in this section.

*Speech 1: Value Creation Theories Relating to Software
Development*

Introduction

As the challenge of finding the appropriate process for the value
creation within an organization is increasing as the
competitiveness increases, it is imperative to consider the
overall value chain in software development projects. An
organization should analyze the specific tasks performed within
the software development process in an effort to measure how
it creates a competitive advantage over other organizations
within the industry. In order to conduct this analysis, it is useful
for an organization to model the organization as a chain of value
generating activities that are identifiable as the value chain
analysis approach created by Michael Porter, according to Evans
and Smith (2004). The goal of the value chain activities is to
produce value that will surpass the actual tangible cost of
generating and producing the actual product or service. The
development of software is a critical role in the support of
creating organizational value along the value chain. This would
include research and development, development process
automation, and other activities along the software
development life cycle that is utilized to support the overall
value chain activities. . Technology development plays an
important role in the support of creating value along the chain
within the organization. This includes research and
development, process automation, and other information
systems creation that is utilized to support the overall value

chain activities. The importance for an organization to understand that improving software development dynamics can maximize value delivery of software products which starts by examining value creation and value capture in the presence of high uncertainty. It is imperative to explore project staffing, optimal release dates, and potential impacts of process improvement. A method to reduce actual costs and to maintain high quality includes the outsourcing of software programming tasks to firms that specialize in the specific programming expertise. This outsourcing arrangement includes firms that are located offshore, such as India.

The Concept of Value Chain Analysis

The value chain analysis is the process that evaluates and synthesizes the sequential value-creating activities and it is the amount that the buyers are willing to pay for the product or service that is provided by an organization. The extent that the value exceeds the total costs required to build the product or service to the ultimate customer is the nature of the profitability recognized by the organization. The primary activities within Michael Porter's value chain include inbound logistics, operations, outbound logistics, marketing and sales, and service. The inbound logistics is the first of the primary activities within the value chain, which is an activity involving the receiving, storing, and distribution of raw materials (inputs) to the final products or service, according to Evans and Smith. In order to evaluate this value chain activity, the organization would review the raw material and inventory control systems and measure the overall effectiveness and efficiency of the process. The operations activity deals with the assurance that the plant operations are efficient, an appropriate level of automation is utilized, quality control is employed, and

workflow designing is efficient which ensures the proper
transformation of the raw materials (inputs) into the final
created merchandise or serviceable use. The outbound logistics
is linked to the collection, storing, and distribution of the final
product or service that is done by reviewing the shipping
process. Cuffe (2005) presents that the marketing and sales
activity is associated with the inducements involved with
promotion of getting consumers to actually pay for the product
or service being produced. The last primary activity on the value
chain deals with the area of service that should improve or
preserve the overall value of the final product or service, which
Cuffe indicates how technology improves the value through
improved data mining techniques available.

According to Hsiao and Ormerod (1998), the provision for value
is consistently changing where technology enables
organizations to develop from the value added to value
generating considering the digital economy and its overall
impact on the evolution of value theory. Technology is one of
the supporting activities along the value chain that have
dramatic impact on each of the value chain components.
Dessureault, Porter, and Woodhall (2004, January) presents that
information technology has become a key source of productivity
and the information technology infrastructure is critical to
achieve productivity improvements throughout the entire value
chain. As the growth of internet and electronic commerce
continues, it is becoming more important to maximize the
competitive advantage by exploiting the opportunities afforded
by the web and technological advances. Evans and Smith states
that there has been a growing focus in aligning strategies that
foster the competitive advantages that are based on Porter's

value chain model and further identifies Internet as a new business channel. The technology component should be seen more than just a supporting component as it currently appears to be a potential instrument to augment the value chain's primary components and reflects how the integration can actually generate a useful tool for the improvement of competitive advantage.

The Role of Software Development in the Value Chain Analysis

The development of software has played a critical role within the value chain of an organization in many various factors, according to Saran (2007, October 20). Technology development is one of the four support activities of the value chain and it is related to a wide range of activities and can actually be incarnated in the actual processes, equipment, and the product itself. In an effort to measure software development activities, the organization should consider the following components: (a) systems analysis activities for the developmental initiatives, (b) positive collaboration between the information systems group and the business user, (c) organizational culture to improve creativity and innovation of software designs, (d) IT professional qualifications, and (e) the ability to meet deadlines and quality on the delivery of software development projects.

Donlan (2007, March) discusses the importance of the interaction and relationships of the systems development team among the value chain activities is critical and urgent as both the software development side and business side of the organization must be aligned. Failure to align these two divisions will have an effect on the attainment of the overall mission and vision of the organization in their strategic initiatives. The internal analysis perspective of software generation deals with phenomena within the organization and the external analysis perspective deals with the involvement within the industry and its competitive environment. The software generation activities are often involved in innovative production processes, trade secrets, patents, trademarks, and copyrights that can be viewed as tangible resources within the organization. An example of this includes Carnival Cruise Lines, where the reservations core system that is encircled by state-of-the-art technology creates a competitive advantage with its pioneering production and service processes within the cruise line industry. The core reservations system was custom made and written in-house to ensure its copyright design. The core system has been adapted to handle new technology by building interfaces to the various technological advances such as hand-held devices, internet booking, and other such technologies.

The Evolution of the Value Chain Analysis Concept in Software Development

According to Pil and Holweg (2006), the evolution of the value chain analysis concept grew in 1985 from the promotion of Michael Porter when he authored a book about building competitive advantage. It began as a theory that grouped the generic value adding primary and support activities within a particular organization, but has now extended beyond that of individualized organizations as it is often now applied to the whole supply chain and distribution networks affecting the organization as a whole.

The ultimate delivery of products or services to the end user often involves several different economic factors and having its own manageable value chain, as presented by Buss (2007, March). The coordinated relations and exchanges within the organizational value chain can move away from the typical local value chains in the past and even extend across the world through the globalization of business activities, becoming a larger interrelated system of value chains. Buss further calls this value system and it plays an important role in the new approach of the value chain analysis. Pil and Holweg further adds that this new approach is lead by the determination of methods to exploit upstream and downstream information flowing along the value chain in order to bypass the intermediaries creating processes to improve the overall value system.

Software generation activities are part of the overall IT supporting role of the value chain, which means that the participants in software generation will play a critical role in this new approach of the value chain by their determination of methods to exploit the upstream and downstream information process. This includes all aspects of the software development life cycle and processes include requirements gathering, system design, and use of automated software engineering tools, system building tasks, quality control, implementation, and maintenance. With regards to system building tasks such as program coding, the use of outsourcing offshore has become a viable option to generating quality and reducing overall cost. We will first explore the value creation theories relating to software development and then its ultimate integration to the **outsourcing of various software development tasks.**

The Value Chain Theory in Software Development

According to Johnson (2006, Summer), alignment of strategic planning and decision making between IT and business leaders

is required for an organization's economic standing and
survivability in the long run. The author indicated that the
leaders should create strategic initiatives that are unique to
their own business and not generic in nature. IT and business
management can carry out this value adding process by
identifying the software development requirements and
analyzing the business processes based on a top-down analysis
of actual software needs and relationships within their
engineering strategic initiatives. The ultimate goal in creating
value is to have the software generation team work with
business management to focus software development activities
on the global needs of the organization, which depend on the
following: (a) top management involved in identifying projects
required for long term production and marketing plans (two of
the primary activities on the value chain), (b) establishment of a
steering committee to deal with the organization's strategic
objectives (covers most of the primary value chain functions),
and (c) the involvement of the user department stakeholders in
development tasks of software generation to ensure
departmental needs are met (all value chain functions).

This increase in the value chain from software development can
be obtained through four significant components: (a) the
introduction of computer-aided software engineering (CASE)
tools, (b) proper management alignment between IT and
business strategies, (c) appropriate employment of an adequate
system development methodology, and (d) proper allocation of
people resources through the life cycle. According to Porter
(2001, March), CASE tools provide the automated support for
the development of software and are designed to support the
tasks that occur over the multiple phases of the systems

development life cycle. It includes the use of a repository to store all diagrams, forms, and report definitions. These tools provide for the automated generation of program code and database definition from the artifacts stored within the repository. The tools also allow for the improved efficiency of managing the project, collection of user requirements, designing system interfaces, controlling defects, testing software, and implementation tasks. CASE tools are designed specifically to support activities that often occur over multiple phases of a software development project.

According to Johnson (2006), strategic planning and decision making is required for an organization economic standing and survivability in the long run. The author further states that the leaders should generate a strategy that is unique to their own business. With this in mind, it is critical to ensure the software generation planning and the overall business strategies are properly aligned. According to Buxbaum (2001, May 7), business and technology have become increasingly intertwined and it is becoming a significant organizational issue. This author has stated that software development has emerged from the back room to the forefront of the corporate world, especially in the rise of an e-commerce economy. The potential effectiveness, efficiency, and competitive advantages that software development and other integrated technology can bring forth have made such an alignment even more crucial. The objective of any organization is to achieve a competitive advantage over other organizations within the industry in which it exists. This can be accomplished in a significant manner, once the software development strategies are aligned with business strategies. Johnson (2006) suggests that the definition and purpose of strategy and its proper alignment is critical to maintain viability, competitiveness, and leadership.

It is important to have the appropriate employment of an adequate system development methodology. According to Boehm (2006), the software development process, along with its associated systems analysis and design phase, needs to be more adaptive as the business community advances into the future economy. The process of software development has progressed through three significant phases, which include: (a) developer-as-artist, (b) developer-as-engineer, and (c) agile methodologies. The first of these phases in software development, developer-as-artist, was evidenced by software developers not documenting the programs being developed or did not utilize development tools during the development process. The software developers in this phase were considered geniuses and artists as a high degree of dependence on the software developer was necessary for continued maintenance. The next phase, developer-as-engineer, was when organizations brought more control and regulation to the software development arena as the development process and the life cycle of software development became a more structured process. This is where the rise of a waterfall system development methodology was formed where the system development life cycle is more of a linear process and moves in strict order from the actual software system concept, through the software system design, implementation, testing, installation, troubleshooting, and finally ends up with the ultimate operation and maintenance of the software system. The rise of the third phase, agile development methodologies, has been ushered in the last few years as the growth of the

Internet economy and object-oriented approach have intersected, according to Yu, Wang, Zhang, Barksdale, and Yuan (2006). Agile software development methodologies require closer cooperation between programmers and the ultimate business user community, it combines a number of software life cycle phases into fewer phases, and involve multiple iterations of software implementations within an application system. Prototyping, time constraints, smaller project team members, management involvement, and iterative software development are all significant components of the agile software developmental process. This new concept of agile software development has aided in the value adding to software generation and seems to fit into a world where the requirements for businesses to develop application software at a faster pace in order to meet the demands of a changing environment. There are several alternative agile software developmental approaches that add significant value to the software development process, according to Olague, Etzkorn, and Gholston (2007, June), including Rapid Application Development, Crystal family, Adaptive Software Development, Scrum, Feature Driven Development, and eXtreme Programming. These agile methods generally share three basic characteristics: (a) focus development of software on the adaptive process rather than predictive methodologies, (b) focus on human resources and individual skills (business and developer) rather than roles, and (c) a self-adaptive process. The agile software generation process can add to the overall value chain when the software development project involves: (a) unpredictable or dynamic software system requirements, (b) responsible and motivated software developers, and (c) users who understand and will get involved.

The proper allocation of human resources through the life cycle is another critical component to adding to the value chain. In an effort to increase the value of software development, an organization should look at the way they recruit software development staff, the process in developing software programming staff, and procedures in retaining software developers. A software developer should be hired based on his or her general knowledge and experience (enough experience but general enough to adapt to changes), social skills (needed for interface with users), values, beliefs, and attitudes. According to Carayannis and Alexander (1999, August), human capital in software generation based upon capabilities, knowledge, skills, and experience help create value of the software generation group in this knowledge intensive economy. This requires sound recruiting practices involving the scanning process of available programming candidates with the challenge of finding the right job candidates, not the greatest number of candidates. In order to develop the human capital for software generation; human resources in IT should be trained and developed at all levels, accounting for the rapid changes in technology so that programming skills do not become obsolete. These resources should be developed to ensure that the developers and users share knowledge and work together in an effort to reach organizational objectives. It is important to provide mechanisms that prevent the transfer of valuable and sensitive information to the outside of the organization by identifying with its mission and values. This is done by building a strong alliance to the organization, providing challenging work, stimulating the environment, and incentives that are tied to quality work performed. Exodus of quality programming resources can have a tremendous effect on software development activities and can erode an organization's competitive advantage.

Due to need to adapt to a more agile software development environment and to reduce costs of human resources while maintaining quality, outsourcing of software programming activities have become a possible solution to add value to software generation activities. Some organizations find a shortage of quality software programmers that meet both skills of new technologies that are cost-effective. According to Sullivan (2004, July), an organization that outsource programming resources offshore to countries such as India will typically save anywhere from sixty to seventy percent on overall development costs.

The Integration of Value Creation of Software Development to Outsourcing

As one looks at the increasing popularity of agile programming methodologies for software development projects and the need to reduce software development costs, the outsourcing of software generation activities have become an effective and efficient way to add to the value chain. According to Mojsilovi, Ray, Lawrence, and Takriti (2007, December), the reasons that offshore outsourcing has grown include two primary values added: (a) significant reduced costs and (b) reduced time to market which fits the agile development methodology. The costs, according to Davis, Ein-Dor, King, and Tarkzadeh (2006), can vary between twenty-five percent to sixty-five percent depending on the complexity of the software generation project and the length of time that both organization and offshore outsourcing firm have worked together. The longer both firms work together the closer to sixty-five percent, or even seventy percent in some cases, in cost savings can be realized. This adds significant value to an organization. Offshore outsourcing of programming to locations of India, Russia, and China have shown many benefits to the organizational value chain as it relates to overall software development, including cost savings, reduced time to market, and the ability to quickly extend an organization's current capabilities at a much lower capital risk than using domestic human resources. Agile programming requires the ability to adapt programming resources quickly, effectively, and efficiently. Offshore outsourcing generally will offer a more transparent way to adapt human resources to these methods at a reduced cost and more flexibility towards agile programming.

According to Davis, Ein-Dor, King, and Tarkzadeh, outsourcing software development has reflected in economic savings and the exact amount will depend on how much is outsourced and the overall effectiveness of the relationship between organization and the outsourcing partner. By reducing capital requirements, programming resource costs, and operation costs through effective software development outsource agreements, the value of generated software is increased significantly. Technology is constantly changing making it difficult for organization's IT departments to train programming staff fast enough to keep up with new technological advances. By outsourcing these human resources, an organization can take advantage of the technological advances with little capital investment allowing for increased productivity on core expertise already existing within the IT department. While many countries have been involved with outsourcing contracts including Russia, Ukraine, and China, one can look at India as being the leaders in the programming outsource contracts, according to Davis, Ein-Dor, King, and Tarkzadeh. The discovery is that the human resources are plentiful and India is the world's second largest highly populated country. With heavy investment in training highly qualified and technically skilled programming professionals that are capable of speaking English with the clients in the United States, India has the lead in the field of offshore IT outsourcing abilities. Additionally, India has a government structure that fully supports IT by helping in the improvement of the necessary infrastructure required for outsourcing contracts, including communication. Mir and Mir (2005, December) states that the Indian government provides great support for the software firms in this provision of infrastructure, basic facilities, favorable policies toward IT companies, and other supportive aspects that has aided in India leading the offshore IT outsourcing business. This includes reliable satellite and submarine communication links that engages India IT outsourcing firms to have excellent band connectivity with their clients and the entire globe. Another factor that favors India is the difference in time zones. While the organization in the United States is asleep, the programmers in India are busy working through the organizations night since it is daylight in India. This allows for overnight delivery of software programming activities, adding value for maintenance of completed software or fixing programming changes on the fly. In consideration of these advantages of outsourcing portions of IT tasks, it is imperative to explore how outsourcing can assist in project staffing, optimal release dates, and potential impacts of process improvement.

How Outsourcing Offshore adds the Value in Human Resources

As previously stated, in an effort to increase the value of software development, an organization should look at the way they recruit software development staff, the process in developing software programming staff, and procedures in retaining software developers. Outsourcing offshore is a method of recruiting the right human resources at the best cost by ensuring the programming resources have enough experiences to easily adapt to the rapid business changes along with updated skills and experiences to handle newer technologies and an attitude for a quality job. The developmental responsibility of the programming staff is passed to the outsourcing firm and no longer becomes a burden to the organization and reduces training costs. As long as there is a good rapport between the organization and the outsourcing firm, the retaining of software developers will become established.

Offshore outsourcing of IT related services, such as programming, has been a growing trend in many organizations and will most likely continue. One might expect that this trend will continue due to the advantages of an offshore programming service procurement contract. These advantages include cost savings and the allowance for an organization's project team to focus on other critical project activities such as requirements definition and system validation efforts. The significant cost savings are realized by having access to lower cost economies such as India. This is caused by the wage gap that exists between industrialized (United States) and developing nations (India). This in itself will add value to the software generation process. Additional benefits of outsourcing portions of technology include a sense of cost restructuring involving the changing of the fixed costs to a variable costs ratio. This is done by transferring normal fixed costs of housing services such as programming to the offshore outsource firm, converting these into variable costs. The outsourcing agreements achieve improved quality by including a service level agreement to the outsource contracts. Additionally, the training costs of programmers are reduced as the access to wider experiences and knowledge are easily acquired through the transfer of this responsibility to the outsource firm, presenting an automatic access to a larger talent pool with various source of skills and talents. Considering all of these benefits of offshore outsourcing of various IT resources, the value creation can be greatly increased when portions of the system development life cycle includes an outsource agreement.

Conclusion

The concept of value creation through technology is heavily dependent upon the alignment of technology and business strategies. While the value creation for an organization is a network of relationships between internal and external environments, technology plays an important role in improving the overall value chain of an organization. However, this increase requires business and technology management to work as a creative, synergistic, and collaborative team instead of a purely mechanistic span of control. Technology can help the organization recognize improved competitive advantage within the industry it resides and generate superior performance at a greater value. Consideration of using agile development approaches, outsourcing of portions of the software development activities, and true alignment between business

and technology strategies are key to recognizing value in
software generation projects.

As the challenge of finding the appropriate process for the value
creation within an organization is increasing and as the
competitiveness increases, it is imperative to consider the
overall value chain in software development projects. An
organization should analyze the specific tasks performed within
the software development process in an effort to measure how
it creates a competitive advantage over other organizations
within the industry. In order to conduct this analysis, it is useful
for an organization to model the organization as a chain of value
generating activities that is identifiable as the value chain
analysis approach created by Michael Porter. The goal of the
value chain activities is to produce value that will surpass the
actual tangible cost of generating and producing the actual
product or service. The development of software is a critical
role in the support of creating organizational value along the
value chain. This would include research and development,
development process automation, and other activities along the
software development life cycle that is utilized to support the
overall value chain activities. . Technology development plays
an important role in the support of creating value along the
chain within the organization. This includes research and
development, process automation, and other information
systems creations that are utilized to support the overall value
chain activities. There is an importance for an organization to
understand that improving software development dynamics can
maximize value delivery of software products. It starts by
examining value creation and value capture in the presence of
high uncertainty within the highly competitive marketplace. It is

imperative to explore project staffing, optimal release dates, and potential impacts of process improvement. A method to reduce actual costs and to maintain high quality includes the outsourcing of software programming tasks to firms that specialize in the specific programming expertise. This outsourcing arrangement includes firms that are located offshore, such as India.

Speech 2: Let us Go Agile: eXtreme Programming and Dynamic **Systems Development Method**

Introduction

According to Boehm (2006), the software development process, along with its associated systems analysis and design phase, needs to be more adaptive as the business community advances into the future economy. It is apparent that the process of software development has progressed through three significant phases, which include: (a) developer-as-artist, (b) developer-as-engineer, and (c) agile methodologies. The first of these phases in software development, developer-as-artist, was evidenced by software developers not documenting the programs being developed or did not utilize automated tools during the development process. The software developers in this phase were considered geniuses and artists as a high degree of dependence on the software developer was necessary for continued maintenance. The next phase, developer-as-engineer, was when organizations brought more control and regulation to the software development arena as the development process and the life cycle of software development became a more structured process. This is where the rise of a waterfall system development methodology was formed in which the system development life cycle is more of a linear process and moves in strict order from the actual software system concept, through the software system design, implementation, testing, installation, troubleshooting, and finally ends up with the ultimate operation and maintenance of the software system. The rise of the third phase, agile development methodologies, has been ushered in over the last few years as the growth of the Internet economy and object-oriented approach have intersected. Agile software development methodologies require closer cooperation between programmers and the ultimate business user community, combines a number of software life cycle phases into fewer phases, and involve multiple iterations of software implementations within an application system. Prototyping, time constraints, smaller project team members, management involvement, and iterative software development are all significant components of the agile software developmental process. This new concept of agile software development has aided in adding value to software generation and seems to fit into a world where the requirements for businesses to develop application software are at a faster pace in order to meet the demands of a changing environment.

According to Meso & Jain (2006), the development of a business application system for software has traditionally followed a non-adaptable waterfall methodology and can take a large amount of time to complete the project. As a result of today's turbulent business strategies there is a need for software development methodologies that are much more adaptable in order to be consistent with the increasing business change requirements, as presented by these authors. To allow for adaptability, agile software development methodologies have been developed. Two such methodologies are eXtreme Programming and Dynamic Systems Development Method.

The Rise of Agile Development Methodologies

As organizations move into the future economy, Boehm states that software systems analysis and design process needs to an overall as it moves from the traditional developer-as-engineer process to become a more agile process. With the traditional developer as an engineer approach being a structured process with control and regulation, it is tough to adapt to the rapid changes as a result of turbulent business competitiveness. The competitiveness in many industries has created this turbulent environment because of the intersection of the Internet economy and the object-oriented technology, opening the door to agile development methodologies. With the requirements for organizations to develop application software systems at a faster pace in order to achieve the demands of a shifting business environment, agile development methodologies have commanded attention of IT management. According to Shenhar, Milosevic, Dvir, and Thamhain (2007, September), agile methodologies require better strategic alignment between IT management and business community management as it combines numerous system life cycle phases into less phases having many iterations of software deployments. Prototyping, iterative development, time constraints, smaller project teams, and active management involvement are all significant elements of agile software development methodology.

For the most part, agile methodologies share three basic commonalities according to Nord and Tomayko (2006, March/April) that include: (a) an adaptive focus instead of predictive methods, (b) a team member approach as individuals instead of pre-defined roles, and (c) leads towards a more self-adaptive process. Turk, France, and Rumpe (2005, October-December) states that an agile process should be considered for software development projects that are: (a) unpredictable or dynamic requirements, (b) self-motivated and talented developers, and (c) a user community that understands the need to be involved in the entire system development life cycle. In contrast, a more traditional, structured methodology is recommended when the development team is large and the project has a fixed price and scope contract, distinguished by project size, dynamism, project membership, criticality, and culture. Agile development methodology is an umbrella term that refers to an alternative approach to system development including eXtreme Programming and Dynamic Systems Development Method.

eXtreme Programming as an Agile Method

eXtreme Programming (XP) is an agile methodology to software development that requires a disciplined attitude among its project team members and has been utilized by many organizations of various sizes globally, according to Cowham and Stephens (2005, March). XP is a methodology of software development that has seen success due to its emphasis on quality and user satisfaction by delivering software to meet user requirements and needs in a timely fashion. XP allows the software developer to confidently respond to changing business user requirements, even though they may be late within the systems development life cycle. This methodology generally emphasizes project team members to work together as a team and not an individual, forgetting the traditionalized roles of more traditional software development methods. Management, the user community, and software developers are all part of a development team that is dedicated to delivering quality software in a timely manner as XP provides a simple and effective method to enabling a groupware development style. According to Cowham and Stephens, XP appears to improve the software development project in four ways: (a) better communications between user and developers, (b) simplicity in

its project tasks, (c) feedback among the project team members
(business and technology), and (d) courage to complete the
software project due to being more cohesive among the
business and technology sides of the organization.

XP was introduced as a response to handle turbulent business
environments whose business user requirements change rapidly
and the actual users generally do not have a firm grip as to what
they actually need systematically to meet competition within
their organizational industry. Layman, Williams, and Damian
(2006, September) states that there are many software
development environments in many industries that reflect
dynamically changing of business user requirements are the
only constant factor on the project, as the application system
may be expected to change often to fit industrial and
competitive expectations. XP processes are designed to mitigate
the risk of developing software to meet changing system
requirements within a shortened defined implementation date
to meet market demands within the industry that the
organization resides in. The increase of possible success, as
described by Hilkka, Tuure, and Matti (2005, October-
December), comes from the setting up of small groups of
programmers, usually between two and thirty programmers.
While ordinary programmers are capable of utilizing XP, it is
important to keep the development team of programmers small
as this methodology does not work with a huge programming
staff. As a matter of fact, Hilkka, Tuure, and Matti recommend
limiting the number of programmers to twelve. This
methodology requires an extended development team of
managers and user participants working together in harmony,
asking questions, collaborating on the scope, settling on

schedules, and testing functionality of the software as it is completed within its iteration. Testability of completed iterations of software is important in XP and the use of an automated unit and functional testing scripts are critical to the success of an XP software development project. The involvement of management and users in XP projects generally reflects more software developer productivity when compared to the traditional methods within the same organizational environment, according to Layman, Williams, and Damian. The objective of XP is to complete and implement software that the business user needs at the point in time that it is actually needed.

The first part of following an XP methodology is to consider the planning portion of the iterative software development project, which starts by preparing user stories. While these user stories have the same purpose of use cases, they differ by the fact that there is not a large requirements document and are not limited to describing user interfaces. These user stories are written by the user within their own terminology that simply describes what they need the application system to do for them. The users with the aid of the programmers will ensure that most of the application system's functionality is desired and is included within the user stories, which should be reviewed and approved by management to ensure that the organizational objectives are being met. Then a release planning meeting is conducted to create a system software release plan that generates the objectives for the implementation schedule of each individual user story created. This small implementation is called "iteration." Bisson (2004, November 4) states that it is critical for technical people to make the decisions required for technical issues and business users to be concerned with project issues related to business. Once the user stories are analyzed and time frames formed, the user community will then prioritize the importance for each iteration to be designed, developed, tested, and deployed.

The designing portion must be kept simple and will often involve the use of Class, Responsibilities, and Collaboration Cards that aid in the design of the application as a team in an object oriented environment. The use of these types of cards will aid in the overall design of the application system by involving more individuals and having the larger number of ideas being incorporated within the overall design. The class of the object would be placed on the top of the card, responsibilities included on the left side of the card, and the collaborating classes presented next to each responsibility within the right side of the card. The removal of redundancy, unused functionality, and obsolete designs are important in the XP process and should be conducted throughout the entire software project life cycle, according to Cowham and Stephens, in an effort to reduce developmental time and improve overall quality of the completed application system. This is a method to keep the overall design simple and avoid unnecessary complexity or redundancy that could be programming nightmares in the future maintenance or enhancement of the application system.

The actual coding of the software application system must still involve the user community and must be written to pre-approved and agreed upon standards. The programming code that will be part of the production release should be generated by two individuals working together at a single workstation, which is called pair programming. Zin, Idris, and Subramamian

(2006, Summer) states that this type of pair programming will ultimately increase application and software quality without having a big impact on the project delivery time. Two individuals at one workstation will add as much functionality as two working separately but with much higher quality as two individuals working together will have the benefit of utilizing each other's creativity traits. This will bring large savings in the long run of the project. Canfora, Cimitile, Garcia, Piattini, and Visaggio (2007, August) presents the fact that pair programming involves one individual to type and think tactically about the program being generated and developed, while the other individual will consider how the program will fit into the object class. After coding is completed on a particular class object, the code must be unit tested followed by acceptance testing. The user community is heavily involved in all testing efforts and these testing scenarios are usually written by the user during the design portion as the user stories are completed. When a defect is noted through the testing efforts, the problem must be concisely defined by the business user and effectively communicated by the programmers with an acceptance test plan written. This will be utilized to ensure the defect has been fixed and it is ready for the production environment.

The significant factor of XP is that the development team of business user software must be able to release iterative versions of the application system software to the users often in order to be effective and efficient. This is accomplished by the prioritization of business function components and releasing the small units of functionality that makes the best business sense to be released into the users' production environment early in the project. The longer the development team waits to deploy important functionality, the greater the risk of having less time to fix problems that may arise due to misunderstandings or changing requirements due business environmental issues.

In summary, XP is an agile software development methodology that embodies and encourages communication, simplicity, feedback, courage, and respect within the development team of programmers, management, and business users. It is an attempt to reconcile human resources and productivity as a path to improvement of business user application systems within a pre-defined discipline. While the traditional development processes have requirements determined at the beginning of the project, the requirements are generally shaped and molded during the entire developmental stage of each iterative unit. XP is a developmental methodology that is more flexible with business user changes and reduces the cost of these changes through discipline, values, principals and practices. The adaptability of changing business requirements throughout the system development life cycle is considered more realistic and a better approach to business units with changing needs than to define all requirements at the beginning of the project which forces change control procedures to be introduced. Change control procedures that are a part of traditional methods are eliminated with the introduction of XP.

Dynamic Systems Development Method as an Agile Method

Howard (1997) states that the Dynamic Systems Development Method (DSDM) is a popular approach to application software development that utilizes continuous business user involvement which responds to the business changing requirements in a more adaptive approach through the iterative development process. While some may argue with the origins of this agile methodology, it appears to have its roots from the 1980's where James Martin created an application development process that was more than programming. According to Howard, Rapid Application Development (RAD) was created to present a higher level of responsibility that includes both a business unit requirement capturing and testing. RAD was an actual response to meet the constant changing business needs that the non-agile methodologies such as the typical waterfall methodology developed in the 1970's had difficulty handling. According to Calvert (1996, June 5), the issue with previous methodologies, such as the waterfall method, was that the development of application systems that took a long time to construct and its requirements would be changed by the user group prior to the application system being completed, which resulted in systems that were not suitable for use. Beginning with the ideologies of Barry Boehm and Scott Shultz, James Martin created RAD at IBM in the late 1980's with a formalization of this agile methodology in his book published in 1991, according to Howard (1997). The principal aspect of RAD is that it will combine the utilization of computer aided software engineering (CASE) tools, rapid prototyping, and joint application design with significant user involvement throughout the process. This methodology decreases the time required to design and deploy software by combining the traditional system development life cycle phases and the actual iteration is generally restricted to design and development phases. According to Eva (2001, December), there are five principal factors that are required to be instituted within the overall development process in order to make RAD a success, which include: (a) extensive business user involvement, (b) joint application design sessions involving users, management, and developers, (c) prototyping, (d) integrated CASE tools, and (e) code generators. Accordign to Howard, RAD is not really a single agile methodology but more of a general strategy that meets the following objectives: (a) analyze business processes rapidly, (b) design viable application system solution through significant cooperation between users, management, and developers, and (c) getting the finished software application system into the hands of the business users rapidly.

This approach includes four factors to ensure success which includes people, CASE tools, methodology, and management. Howard states that individuals on the project development team should include a small number of members and be comprised of experienced, motivated, and versatile individuals that are capable of performing several various functions. CASE tools provide the automated support for the system process as they are designed to support project tasks that are performed over multiple phases of the system life cycle such as code generators and data base definitions, along with the utilization of a repository to store all diagrams, forms, and report definitions. Use case analysis, testing scenarios, prototyping of forms, and joint application design sessions that will aid in the process of involving the user throughout the development stages. Management support and involvement are important in order to make RAD a success.

Out of the development of RAD, Dynamic Systems Development Method (DSDM) was created as an agile methodology framework in England in the 1990's by a group of vendors and experts, according to Howard (1997). The objective of this method was to create an agile development method by combining several best practice experiences and has been adapted over the years with the last version completed in 2003, as presented by Avdin, Harmsen, van Slooten, and Stegwee (2005, October - December). Like RAD, it utilizes continuous business user involvement that requires nine significant principles, according to Andrea and Elias (2007, April - June). This includes the following principles: (a) business user involvement, (b) empowered software project team, (c) frequent delivery of software iterations (functional components), (d) delivering an application system that meets the current user requirements, (e) iterative and incremental development, (f) reversible changes, (g) a higher level of scope and requirements at the beginning of the project, (h) testing is carried out throughout the entire project life cycle, and (i) communication and cooperation among all project stakeholders is evident.

According to Balmelli, Brown, and Cantor (2006, July), there must be an acceptance of DSDM by senior manager and all other stakeholders. The mechanics of the methodology includes the systems requirement determination in the context of a joint business user and system developers to discuss the high level of business problems and areas of concern. Then, the user's design phase which includes the business users and developers participate in joint application design sessions and prototyping activities. The construction phase is started with the designer creating code by utilizing code generators and finish with the business user validation of forms, reports, dialogue boxes, and other such aspects of design. The final part of the process is to cut over the final iteration of the system's functional component by deploying it into the production environment as a delivery to the end business user community. A visual display

of this agile methodology based on the scholarly writing of
Howard is reflected as follows:

In similarity to XP, DSDM are related in that it delivers two
primary advantages of increased speed and quality of
applications being developed. However, DSDM distinguishes
itself by the fact that it provides for a technique of independent
framework, as XP has specific methods or processes. This allows
for the team members to complete the specific tasks of the
methodology with their own techniques and software aids of
choice in an effort to meet the time and cost constraints. Like
most agile methodologies, the significant objective of DSDM is
that a strong communication and stakeholder involvement is
required to ensure a successful outcome of the software
project.

Compelling Justification of Agile Software Development

There is much justification of agile software development
methods such as RAD, DSMD, and eXtreme Programming.
According to Meso & Jain, the principal characteristic of agile
software development methods is that it makes programming
application software more rapid as it tends to combine the
utilization of CASE tools, rapid prototyping, and Joint
Application Design, with heavy user or ultimate customer
involvement throughout the process. The development process
in agile software development differs with the traditional
System Development Life Cycle (SDLC) by having each
component within the application project in different phases
during the project-life cycle. According to Calvert (1996, June 5),
the rapid development of these agile methodological
procedures, the non-traditional techniques of agile processes,

and the need to understand the best attributes to ensure success in agile software development have all contributed to the rise and compelling argument to support this software development approach. This has opened the doors for additional study of the project management research of this new seminal knowledge of software development, with the ultimate objective of each study is to create more knowledge of this project management approach in software development. Several of the agile development methodologies have been argued to be a solution to many of the problems that continue to affect software development projects, and it is important to understand that the seminal research in these types of study have conducted an evaluation and synthesis of the case studies involved to determine the best agile approach and appropriate characteristics to include ensuring agile development success. The two approaches evaluated not only reflect the most popular of these agile methodologies, but reflect the true spirit of agile software developmental practices. These researchers have formulated their operative paradigm by using research study activity in which the results last as long as the research activity last and is a premise to lead to the meta-theories for the construction of the new realty perception that are important starting points to continued research. The authors utilized case studies to directly observe the process or utilize questionnaire/interview approach.

The utilization of the case study approaches by these researchers of agile development techniques allowed for a more qualitative approach. The researchers had a more in-depth examination of either a single occurrence or samples of multiple occurrences. In many cases the objectivity of this approach was created by the authors and were questioned and changed while they were conducting their research studies. Each researcher started with a thesis, antithesis, and follows with a synthesis where the authors of each study were able to create knowledge.

The researchers in a majority of the researched articles have generally concluded after analyzing and synthesizing the results that the delivery of working, tested, and deployable software on an incremental basis will increase value and adaptability much earlier in the lifecycle while significantly reducing the project risk. The agile systems development approach can be utilized to decrease the time needed to complete the design and radically deploy application systems. There are two primary advantages to this approach which includes the increased speed and quality of applications development process. The two chief disadvantages include reduced scalability and system features due to time constraints as several features are pushed to later versions to ensure shorter development time. The major components for the agile process are to include prototyping, iterative development, time constraints, smaller team members, and a true management involvement approach. The overall theme of these research articles is that the pace of change in the software development industry is high and individuals continue to go beyond the boundaries of traditional methodologies in order to develop software more effectively and efficiently. Agile methodologies have become the new concept that has brought extreme interest of businesses developing software.

Conclusion

According to Boehm, the software development process, along with its associated systems analysis and design phase, needs to be more adaptive as the business community advances into the future economy. The process of software development has progressed through three significant phases, which include: (a) developer-as-artist, (b) developer-as-engineer, and (c) agile methodologies. The first of these phases in software development, developer-as-artist, was evidenced by software developers not documenting the programs being developed or did not utilize development tools during the development process. The software developers in this phase were considered geniuses and artists as a high degree of dependence on the software developer was necessary for continued maintenance. The next phase, developer-as-engineer, was when organizations brought more control and regulation to the software development arena as the development process and the life cycle of software development became a more structured process. This is where the rise of a waterfall system development methodology was formed where the system development life cycle is more of a linear process and moves in strict order from the actual software system concept, through the software system design, implementation, testing, installation, troubleshooting, and finally ends up with the ultimate operation and maintenance of the software system. The rise of the third phase, agile development methodologies, has been ushered in the last few years as the growth of the Internet economy and object-oriented approach have intersected. Agile software development methodologies require closer cooperation between programmers and the ultimate business user community, combines a number of software life cycle phases into fewer phases, and involve multiple iterations of software implementations within an application system. Prototyping, time constraints, smaller project team members, management involvement, and iterative software development are all significant components of the agile software developmental process. This new concept of agile software development has aided in the value adding to software generation and seems to fit into a world where the requirements for businesses to develop application software at a faster pace in order to meet the demands of a changing environment.

According to Meso & Jain, the development of business application system software has traditionally followed a non-adaptable waterfall methodology and can take a large amount of time to complete the project. As a result of today's turbulent business strategies there is a need for software development methodologies that are much more adaptable in order to be consistent with the increasing business change requirements, as presented by these authors. To allow for adaptability, agile software development methodologies have been developed.

Speech 3: Relationship Between IT and TQM

Introduction

Jabnoun and Sahraoui (2004) outlined the relationship between IT and total quality management (TQM) by considering IT as an enabler of TQM. It is important to consider the role of IT within the organizations' implementation of TQM. The organization's strategy and change process that a TQM strategy implementation can bring, along with the IT initiatives, can be related as co-determinants of an organizational structure. The competitiveness in many industries has created this turbulent environment because of the intersection of the Internet economy and the object-oriented technology. With the requirements for organizations to develop application software systems at a faster pace in order to achieve the demands of shifting business environment, the need for agility, quality, efficiency, and effectiveness during the IT management process, the need to utilize IT as an enabler of TQM has grown.

Considering the organizational complexity in today's business environment, customer or user focus, process organization, and cross-functional teams, the enabling role of IT in a TQM infrastructure must be explored in order to increase value. One must first look at the definition of TQM, importance of TQM in IT, the link of TQM in IT, role of IT in TQM implementation, enabling aspects of IT, and innovative utilization of IT to further enhance the utilization of TQM within today's modern organizations.

The Definition of TQM and the Importance of TQM in IT

TQM is the management of total quality that includes the quality of returning to satisfy shareholder needs, quality of products and services to satisfy customer specific needs and requirements, and quality of life to satisfy the needs of the human resources within the organization. In the IT world, the quality of the completed software development project should satisfy the needs and requirements of the ultimate end user, which in turn, can aid the end user of the software application package to create quality to the ultimate customer of an organization. Basically, an organization should consider the entire supply management approach when employing total quality management. This means that the organization must not only satisfy the needs of customers or end users, but also the customer's customers.

Hill and Collins (1999, January) defines TQM as a management strategy that encourages and stresses the importance of quality in each and every organizational process, including the process to operate in a manner of better communication and teamwork to improve production and the reduction of waste within an organization. This would include IT as part of the team to aid in the implementation of a successful TQM program within an organization. Senior management commitment, organizational employee participation, and IT leadership are key components that can have a great affect on the success or failure of a TQM program. With IT being included as a significant component in today's business environment, one could see that technology can increase efficiency, but efficiency alone does not generate quality. However, the improved reliability, effectiveness, and accuracy that technology can bring to the table have worked with efficiency measures to improve total quality.

According to Hsiao and Ormerod (1998), the provision for value is consistently changing where technology enables organizations to develop from the value added to value generating considering the digital economy and its overall impact on the evolution of value theory. Technology is one of the supporting activities along the value chain that have dramatic impact on each of the value chain components. According to Dessureault, Porter, and Woodhall (2004, January), information technology has become a key source of productivity and the information technology infrastructure is critical to achieve productivity improvements throughout the entire value chain. As the growth of internet and electronic commerce continues, it is becoming more important to maximize the competitive advantage by exploiting the opportunities afforded by the web and technological advances.

Donlan (2007, March) discusses that the importance of the interaction and relationships of the systems development team among the value chain activities is critical and urgent as both the software development side and business side of the organization must be aligned. Failure to align these two divisions will have an effect on the attainment of the overall mission and vision of the organization in their strategic initiatives. The internal analysis perspective of the software generation deals with phenomena within the organization and the external analysis perspective deals with the involvement within the industry and its competitive environment.

It is becoming more evident as the organizations move further within the twenty-first century; TQM is becoming critical for every part within an organization, especially IT, in order to create customer satisfaction at continually lower costs. Quality management in IT can be seen as a process to ensure that all project tasks necessary to design, develop, and implement a software product are effective and efficient with respect to the entire organization's system, objectives, business strategy, and actual measurable performance.

Linking TQM to IT Initiatives

Many individuals today have presented an argument that IT investments are a significant factor for increasing core business productivity and reducing costs. Byrd and Marshall (1997) have presented evidence in their study that reflects positive and significant returns from IT investments in business. Devaraj and Kohli (2000) have found similar evidence in the IT interventions within the hospital environment. On the contradictory side of the argument, Willcocks and Lester (1997) failed to find adequate evidence supporting a significant increase in financial performance or even a competitive advantage within the industry the organization resides within. Based on a review of many studies, top management leadership appears to be one of the significant determinants of a successful TQM implementation and refers to the commitment of senior management in employing and inspiring the TQM approach across the organization. Senior management must accept the responsibility and provide the necessary leadership to motivate all of the organization's employees.

Dr. Akao and Mitzuno developed the quality function deployment approach in the 1960's and their focus was on the quality of new products coming through the development process and later extended to services, according to LeProvost and Mazur (2005). One might wonder why total quality management is still important in the twenty-first century and why it should be considered in IT initiatives. TQM techniques in IT projects have proven to deliver IT deliverables with the highest payback as the projects will end up with the right resources needed and deliver a completed IT project on time and within the cost constraints. Sanchez-Rodriguez, Dewhurst, and Martinez-Lorente (2006) have presented that current IT and TQM theory and practice have positive outcomes within their studies that the use of IT in supporting TQM policies and practices within an organization that generate significant positive gains on operational and quality performance. IT and TQM have a significant impact within most organizations based on these authors' studies in Spain reflecting a model showing IT and TQM jointly adds value to manufacturing organizations. This approach allows organizations to effectively manage scarce resources better and reveals a model that presents a higher probability of success. This model includes: (a) managers should focus on the improvement of operational performance measures, (b) increase the investment in IT to support management leadership, customer focus, supplier relations, workforce management, and data collection, and (c) ensure that the data collected can effectively be transformed into management information and reporting strategies. The improved operational measures would include reduced production cost, faster delivery, improved flexibility, and reduced cycle time. According to the study by Sanchez-Rodriguez, Dewhurst, and Martinez-Lorente, the organizations should concentrate on all of the TQM factors in order to improve the focus of quality performance, including product quality and customer satisfaction.

Role of IT in TQM Implementations

The complementary utilization of technology and TQM can be a reality because both are significant parts of an organizational vision and a long-term strategic plan comprising of several elements. The vision in most organizations is to play a leading role within the industry that comprises its objectives and mission. The strategic plan should be the creation of an organization that has the capacity to exist in a permanent state of change, with the ability to obtain business excellence through improvement and innovation techniques.

Jabnoun and Sahraoui insists that IT systems lay the foundation for the TQM initiative and it is clear that TQM initiatives undertaken by management have focused on the technical concepts like product and process design. Secondary focuses of these quality programs involve stakeholder satisfaction that includes customers, stockholders, employees, and suppliers. Another important focus should include the organizational restructuring and cultural changes that these quality programs often bring. Zadrozny and Ferraxxi (1992) provide that the IT function can play a significant role in the organization's TQM program and initiative through the business strategic, human resources, and technology components. Technology has been increasingly utilized to measure, understand, and improve an organization's level of continuing quality through the application of statistical control, quality function implementation, and the process of real-time data collection techniques, according to Jabnoun and Sahraoui. In this light, IT can be an enabler in the drive for continuous improvement and can be a significant tool that facilitates quality with highly-committed senior management leadership. This is necessary to ensure success of the TQM initiative to accomplish significant changes in organizational culture. IT can deliver quality management reports of processed data that can be utilized for the critical decision making process required in such programs.

Hyde (1992) has noted that TQM generates an organizational change in culture and work flow methodology within the organization in a radical manner. This quality improvement process searches for and implements a radical change in organizational processes to achieve a breakthrough improvement in its products and services. The objective of the involvement of IT is to reorganize the complete flow of data in the major sections within an organization, with the objective of eliminating unnecessary steps. This is necessary within the TQM initiative in order to be more responsive to the future changes caused by a turbulent competitive business environment. The role of IT, according to Dewhurst, Martinez-Lorente, and Sanchez-Rodriguez (2003), includes the identification of processes to reengineer, including the set of activities designed to produce specific output for a particular customer or market by focusing on the customers themselves and the overall outcome. This often involves the use of disruptive technologies that enable the breaking of long held business rules that inhibit organizations from making radical business changes. However, a fundamental factor is management leadership where a participative style is important and the alignment of IT strategies and business strategies must be in congruency.

Grace (2000) presents that IT can play a role by aligning the strategies to ensure that information generated from data collection can (a) be analyzed to the point that management can make an effective decision in a highly competitive industry, (b) a tool to alert management of early recognition of both threats and opportunities, (c) a means to deliver reasonable assessments, and (d) an enabler to create TQM as a way of corporate life through process improvement. The role of IT can provide for the relationships between strategy formulation, implementation, and control which are highly interactive in such quality programs. This involves two types of control, informational and behavioral.

According to Margulius (2005, December 5), IT will play an important role to accomplish the technology strategy within the organization that supports the TQM initiative. This includes the creation of technological strategies to provide for information systems governance for senior management. Information systems governance methodologies have become a replacement for the actual leadership component of the quality management program as organizational management is relying more on analysis, strategy meetings, and formalized decision making techniques which brings together the IT management and business executives (Margulius, p 22). May (2006, January 16) states that the future is all about leadership in the information systems world and the leaders will need to create environments, cultures, and behaviors conducive to growth. A strong leader should be able to deal with this aspect by handling all possible alternatives available without having their hands tied. May continues to state that as the information systems management takes a strong leadership role in the organization, a leader will need to consider the following: (a) lessons learned in order not to repeat the mistakes in the past, (b) assurance to meet the needs of internal and external customers, (c) listen to the advice of those individuals surrounding the leader, and (d) keeping abreast of the technology utilized in the economy and related industry. These indicate some critical key roles that IT plays within TQM initiatives employed by an organization. The leader of IT basically is on the verge to have an opportunity to become the chief enabler of quality management activities by becoming innovative with the technology and aligning it accordingly with business strategic directives.

IT must emphasize the application of principles and techniques of TQM in order to be effective within their actual role within the organization as the enabler. When one considers that TQM is an organizational undertaking to improve the quality of products and services, as it focuses on obtaining continuous feedback for making improvements and refining existing processes over the long term, it becomes more obvious that IT can play an important role. This is done through contemporary governance, such as informational control and behavior control, process improvement, leading the structural adjustment of the organization, and proper alignment of IT and business strategic initiatives.

Corporate Governance and IT Role

Corporate governance include informational control that is concerned with whether or not the organization is using the correct processes and behavioral control that is concerned with whether or not the organization is doing the right steps in the implementation of its strategy as it relates to a quality management program. Both types of control are necessary conditions for the success of TQM and technology must play an important role. Information control deals with quality management initiatives as part of an ongoing process of organizational learning that updates and challenges the assumptions underlying the organization's strategy. The behavioral aspect of corporate governance activities involves a balance between organizational culture, reward systems, and corporate boundary controls. This type of contemporary control system must focus on constantly changing information and must be easily identifiable by management as having potential strategic importance.

According to Fondiler (2005, December 29), a survey of executives revealed that sixty-six percent of the executives described strategic planning at their companies is done on a periodic basis, but all of the respondents said they make decisions regarding strategies throughout the entire year. Fondiler continues to state that most corporations spend a great deal of time in strategic planning, but their efforts generate very few worthwhile decisions, as these companies tend to follow a traditional model which works best with static environments. Considering that TQM requires continuous informational and behavioral control to be successful, by making their strategy planning methods continuous and tied to specific issues as an effort to make better and quicker decisions. The continuous corporate governance planning and monitoring can be aided with the combined help of management accountants and improved technology.

According to Williams (2006, January), management accounting within an organization have the ability to provide significant roles in the overall management process, including: (a) implementation and maintenance of controls, (b) strategic planning and decision making supported by analysis, (c) assurance of effective risk management procedures, and (d) assistance in presenting the tone for ethical practices. While management accountants duties are important in the overall success of the quality management process, their ability to accomplish this is aided with technology provided by the IT division within an organization.

According to Boudreaux (2006, January/February), technology is readily available to provide relevant information that is current and accurate, which in turn will enhance the business reporting process. This author further states that technology create a structure for reporting information that is a model that incorporates all types of data, including significant indicators, instead of a historical snapshot. An organization can automate the processing of business data by utilizing computer software which will cut out the time and cost involved with the manual process of retrieving and comparing information, that will ease the ability to select data, process it, analyze it, store it, and present it automatically in a variety of ways for management. In essence, the overall business performance and measurements involved in the TQM initiatives will be readily available in order to aid managers to make better strategic decisions through the technology introduced by IT management. Batchelor (2005, October) continues to state that metrics is the best method to provide a company's progress in operations, demonstrate accountability, and provide a process to evaluate and improve the current progress. This continuous improvement relies on timely information which IT has the ability to provide a method for a business to understand, react, and bring into line the efforts to the established objectives.

IT systems can easily be designed to empower and control organizational membership by allowing management the ability to access real time information (information control). In this aspect, IT actually provides empowerment to allow for the making of well-informed decisions, as IT can be utilized to create controls and monitor employee behavior (behavior control), allowing for the adoption of a clear strategy of empowerment as they reap the benefits of the TQM initiatives. Communication efforts are also a part of the IT role by providing improved communication links and technological advances.

IT Role in Process Improvement

Within the perspective of TQM, an organization needs to understand that innovation and technological advances is the utilization of new knowledge in an effort to convert the organizational processes in order to create viable products and services. IT must present the latest technology to enhance or replace existing practices, making improvement in the development of products or services, and implementing evolutionary applications within the existing paradigms within a highly competitive environment. Francis (2005, October 25) discusses how disruptive innovation, sometimes called creative destruction, could be adopted to make fundamental changes and make substantial breakthroughs by evoking significant departures from existing practices, as a method to transform or revolutionize an entire industry. Being too rigid in the face of new entrants and approaches in today's ever changing economy, will have drastic effect in the long run and could have a loss in the market share. This is where IT leadership becomes critical in the overall strategically objectives and TQM mix within an organization.

As the growth of internet and electronic commerce continues, it is becoming more important to maximize the competitive advantage by exploiting the opportunities afforded by the web and technological advances. According to Evans and Smith, there has been a growing focus in aligning strategies that foster the competitive advantages that are based on Porter's value chain model and further identifies the Internet as a new business channel. The technology component should be seen as more than just a supporting component because it currently appears to be a potential instrument to augment the value chain's primary components and reflects how the integration can actually generate as a useful tool for the improvement of competitive advantage.

Quality within such a program is consistently a moving target in today's highly competitive environment as products and services must be able to meet the dynamic consumer needs. This includes the IT role in making such process improvements to meet these dynamic needs. As the organization itself needs to be more dynamic, agile development methods in IT must be considered, ushering in the last few years as the growth of the Internet economy and object-oriented approach have intersected. Agile software development methodologies require closer cooperation between programmers and the ultimate business user community, combines a number of software life cycle phases into fewer phases, and involve multiple iterations of software implementations within an application system. Prototyping, time constraints, smaller project team members, management involvement, and shorter software development cycles are all significant components of the agile software developmental process. This new concept of agile software development has aided in the value adding to software generation and seems to fit into a world where the requirements for businesses to develop application software at a faster pace in order to meet the demands of a changing environment.

According to Jabnoun and Sahraoui, IT plays a role in applying process improvement solutions within an organization to aid in the realignment of strategy and operations to see a significant increase in operation performance. IT must utilize its systems analysis group to assess existing processes and evaluate actual value added processes through the utilization of redesign methodologies and techniques that will yield enabling technologies that are flexible and fully supportive of organizational operations. Hill and Collins (1999, January) presents that IT plays a role that provides for streamline processes, improved workflow performance, and ultimately maximizes the benefit of every technology dollar spent during the TQM initiative.

The principal structural characteristics affected by TQM changes employed by an organization requires significant changes in the way organizations operates, which at times will require disruptive technologies that are initiated by IT. The utilization of disruptive technology initiates changes within the industry by eliminating the previous rules of business and competition. A new market disruptive innovation can be a critical component in the TQM process by filling a void in the industry where older technology could not provide. This includes the need to adapt to internet strategies as a critical part in global competition. The disruptive technology introduced by IT can improve the market position and total quality through performance improvements. Often the organizations implement such a TQM process often lack synergy between the IT objectives and the TQM objectives, according to Zadrozny and Ferrazi.

Alignment of IT Objectives and TQM Objectives

According to Zadrozny and Ferrazi, it is suggested that organizations should consider the integration of TQM within the agenda of its strategic planning effort where business strategies are simultaneously developed within the IT strategies. The development of software has played a critical role within the value chain of an organization in many various factors, according to Saran (2007, October 20). Technology development is one of the four support activities of the value chain are related to a wide range of activities and can actually be incarnated in the actual processes, equipment, and the product itself. In an effort to measure software development activities, the organization should consider the following components: (a) systems analysis activities for the developmental initiatives, (b) positive collaboration between the information systems group and the business user, (c) organizational culture to improve creativity and innovation of software designs, (d) IT professional qualifications, and (e) the ability to meet deadlines and quality on the delivery of software development projects.

Donlan (2007, March) discusses the importance of the interaction and relationships of the systems development team among the value chain activities and it is critical and urgent because both the software development side and business side of the organization must be aligned. Failure to align these two divisions will have an effect on the attainment of the overall mission and vision of the organization in their strategic initiatives, and ultimately accomplishing the organization's TQM plan. The internal analysis perspective of software generation deals with phenomena within the organization and the external analysis perspective deals with the involvement within the industry and its competitive environment. According to Johnson (2006, Summer), alignment of strategic planning and decision making between IT and business leaders is required for an organization's economic standing, survivability, and TQM efforts in the long run.

TQM practices appear to aim at the improvement of product quality and business process efficiency, but require IT to play an active role requiring the intertwining of the business and technology strategies. The success and strength of TQM is dependent upon integrating business process reengineering activities and IT directives in such a quality management implementation by an organization. Hence, IT just does not play a role in TQM practices, but enables the overall process.

Conclusion

TQM implementation by an organization aims to improve product quality and business process improvement. This includes the utilization of improved communication technologies, corporate governance monitoring abilities, and operational improvements through the introduction of automation and more effective means of improving production activities. IT plays a role in governance by providing for the technology which plays an important role in succeeding with governance control and its relationship to effective and efficient TQM implementations. Information control deals with quality management initiatives as part of an ongoing process of organizational learning that updates and challenges the assumptions underlying the organization's strategy. The behavioral aspect of corporate governance activities involves a balance between organizational culture, reward systems, and corporate boundary controls. This type of contemporary control system must focus on constantly changing information and must be easily identifiable by management as having potential strategic importance.

It is important to consider the role of IT within the organizations' implementation of TQM. The organization's strategy and change process that a TQM strategy implementation can bring, along with the IT initiatives, can be related as co-determinants of an organizational structure. The competitiveness in many industries has created this turbulent environment because of the intersection of the Internet economy and the object-oriented technology. With the requirements for organizations to develop application software systems at a faster pace in order to achieve the demands of a shifting business environment, the need for agility, quality, efficiency, and effectiveness during the IT management process, the need to utilize IT as an enabler of TQM has grown. Considering the organizational complexity in today's business environment, customer or user focus, process organization, and cross-functional teams, the enabling role of IT in a TQM infrastructure must be explored in order to increase value.

Based on the research of related material, one can conclude that the interaction between IT and TQM initiatives are critical. It has been an enabler of TQM directives. As the organizations employing such initiatives can effectively link their IT investments to quality orientated activities, it is easy to see that IT aids the employees to share task related information, facilitate teamwork, and improve workflow processes. In this way, IT plays an active role in the continuous improvement processes, management governance control activities, and address competitive issues within the industry it resides in as a

method to increase overall customer satisfaction, as well as the
quality throughout the entire supply chain.

Speech 4: Research Methods for IT Project Research

Introduction

As the field of Information Technology (IT) project management has been advancing to face the needs of a turbulent business competitive world, it has grown harder to align IT strategies with that of the constant changing business strategies. The need for research studies to discover better methods and approaches in an effort to better align these two strategies have become important. There are three primary research methodologies that have been utilized to conduct studies in the IT Project Management arena. These research methods include an analytical approach, systems approach, and actor's approach. Depending on the approach utilized in the study of IT Project Management, either a quantitative, qualitative, or mixed research process will be utilized. Each method has a purpose and process, along with issues of bias and limitations. According to Blackler and Brown (1983, July), the research methodologies used are generally dependent upon the paradigmatic assumptions of business research studies, such as managing IT projects. The paradigmatic assumptions within the project management business process are the basic truism that build the IT world based on one's experiences, including the messages one receives from significant figures within one's professional path. Once the paradigm is developed, the business research study can begin with these paradigmatic aspects: (1) the stress of one group of events and facts over another, (2) the attempt to demonstrate agreement between the paradigm and reality, and (3) the further refinement of the paradigm.

As IT project management is the process where a leader will organize and manage resources in such a way that the IT development process can be completed within the defined scope, quality, schedule, and cost constraints. Considering the challenges facing IT project managers in areas of being more agile, tighter budget constraints, need for better alignment to constant changing business strategies, and a highly competitive business environment, it is imperative to discover new process methods that will benefit the IT project manager. These types of research problems can easily become a problem solving activity that can shape an unforeseen uniqueness. Research studies can be viewed as a jigsaw puzzle that requires a solution based on the paradigm it resides in. Researchers in IT project management studies generally use a quantitative approach through the analytical and system research methods or use a qualitative approach through the actor's research method. On occasions, the researcher may use a mixed research approach where both quantitative and qualitative approaches are utilized.

Quantitative Approaches

The analytical approach involves quantitative research techniques, hypothesis, and models in order to come to a scholarly conclusion. This type of research method, knowledge and the observer are mutually exclusive as the reality of the experimentation exists independently of the observers. The analytical approach relies on scientific research in order to arrive at a conclusion after the creation of a hypothesis, assumption, and explanation. The strength of this quantitative approach is that it ultimately provides an objective and linear process in the research attempts, while focusing on the cause and effect of relationships, according to Hara (1995). The weakness is that it usually will fail to consider the changeability and volatility of the IT project management environment and its alignment with business sponsor's strategic plans that can be at a moving target in today's highly competitive environment. The strict analytical and quantitative approach does not measure the subjectivity of the project manager's experiences, knowledge, and skills.

The systems approach is another methodology utilized in the study of IT project management and tends to be more of a results oriented approach that enlarges the causal relationship of the analytical approach to the next level of knowledge. This is done by employing a significant quantitative approach through the development by defining its objective and includes a mechanical, biological, self-organizing, and value-laden model according to Gable (1994, April). The business researcher utilizing this approach will be able to develop the models that best fit the needs of the research allowing for the viewing of different elements. The downside of this approach is that researcher bias on a subject can be developed and problems in reaching a concrete conclusion may result, according to Gable. This can be mitigated by field testing the survey instrument prior to the actual data collection efforts, as well as having another research professional conduct a peer-review of the survey questions. This peer-review process, conducted prior to field testing, would involve the evaluation of survey instrument by other people in a similar field in order to maintain or enhance the quality of the instrument.

Both analytical and systems methodologies depend primarily on quantitative research processes that develop a hypothesis and theories with employment of mathematical models to test the natural phenomena. Gable states that the process of measurement is the heart of quantitative research as ties relationship of the empirical observations with mathematical and scientific expressions. The process will start with the generation of models, theories, and hypothesis of various aspects of IT project management. Then the quantitative researcher will develop instruments utilized for measurement, with strict experimental control and manipulation of variables. The researcher will collect data related to an IT project management issue being tested, create models, analyze data, and evaluate the results. According to Lavin and Johnson (2005, June), this process is often a more iterative procedure as the researcher evaluates the evidence, refine theories and hypothesis, and continue the process until a clear, definite answer to the research question can be arrived and justified.

Example and Application of Quantitative Approach

An example of utilizing quantitative research approach was in the study performed by Taylor (2007, April – June). This research was conducted because there are an increasing number of outsourced and multinational IT projects. The management of risks for these projects is becoming even more important than those IT projects completed at the home office. The researcher measured the existence of various typical risks and correlated it to the specific location. The researcher also measured the project success based on how these typical risks were managed. This type of measurement process resembles a typical quantitative IT project study that falls into the analytical research method. This research involved precise quantitative techniques and hypothesis to arrive at a scholarly conclusion. The actual researcher relied on scientific research in order to arrive at the conclusion after the creation of the hypothesis and the assumptions. The research provided validation of the hypothesis and an explanation of the results.

Another study by Tiwana, Wang, Keil, and Ahluwalia (2007, February) revealed that real options theory is a growing trend in managing IT projects but very little study has been done to test if systematic biases exist. Therefore, these researchers conducted a quantitative study by using data collected from eighty-eight firms and determined the existence of bounded rationality bias in the managers' assessments. This study measured the identifiable conditions under which managers will need to be vigilant about neglecting real options and creating a simple approach for the assessment of real options in IT development projects. This quantitative study resembles a systematic research method as it takes the results oriented approach of the typical analytical approach to the next level. The actual study measured the results and then developed a business model that IT project managers can utilize in the future by defining the objective, organizing the data, and develops a value-laden model based on the quantitative results.

Description of Quantitative Process

Quantitative research studies such as the analytical and systemic methods typically rely on statistical methods. These typically begin from the research collection of primary data based on a theory or hypothesis, followed with the mathematical utilization of various descriptive and inferential statistical methods. This study is conducted usually with relatively large statistically representative samples that will allow for the researcher to make statistical generalizations. The researcher of IT project management studies will study the causal relationships by manipulating the various factors that are assumed to affect the influence of the phenomena of interest, while controlling other variables thought to be relevant to the experimental outcomes.

The quantitative researcher can use telephone surveys, mail surveys, web surveys, on-site surveys, or data entry projects. Telephone surveys or interviews can be an efficient and effective method according to Browne, Kaldenberg, and Brown (1992-1993). These types of surveys tend to reach a large number of participants in a short period of time while obtaining a broader sample. The mailing of surveys can be another effective method to reach potential respondents as questionnaires are mailed to a random selection of a population with the objective of receiving back a high percentage of completed surveys. According to Gable, there is a risk of not receiving the right amount of respondents but the response rates can be improved by using incentives, reminders, and postage-paid business reply envelopes. According to Van Rooij (2007), indicated that the use of web surveys have grown to become a viable process of reaching potential participants on survey related projects. Participants are generally invited to participate in a survey either from an email message or when the participant visits a particular website. The process has become an efficient method of reaching a larger population in a short period of time and the follow up email reminders are a cost-effective method to increase participation. On site surveys are primarily utilized to interview or conduct a survey at the actual premises of IT development or at a particular conference such as a Project Management Institute Conference. This can be used as an effective process, especially at conferences where there is enough respondent traffic. This could be done with a professional interviewer or the use of computerized survey technique which is a more self-administered process. The use of professional interviewer at a conference can open the door to ask for further feedback and additional open-ended questions that can lead a mixed research study of both quantitative and qualitative techniques.

Data entry projects for recordation of quantitative data collected involve the collection of data and having a data entry clerk enter the data with specific validation techniques. This data collection could be conducted via surveys from the telephone, web, or mail. Once the data is collected, it is entered into a database for processing into meaningful research information. In addition to surveys, the primary data can also be collected by reviewing previous artifacts of IT projects to determine relevant data that can be processed.

It is important to understand that the quantitative research for IT project management studies must start with sound data and the method of data collection is important to ensure accuracy, reliability, relevancy, validity, and freedom from as much bias as reasonably possible. The participants must truly represent the target population in question and the selection process is critical. This risk of missing the target can be mitigated with sound statistical sampling techniques. The questions of the research instrument utilized must be clear, to the point, and free from bias issues in order to be useful and present value to the IT project management study. Once the process of data collection has been performed, the application of statistical methods is employed. According to Becker (1998, May), the use of statistics is primarily a mathematical science pertaining to the collection, analysis, explanation, and presentation of data that can be utilized to reach an informed conclusion. It presents the conclusion for testing the hypothesis in a measurable means with tangible results. Descriptive statistics are employed to provide for the description of the fundamental characteristics of the data collected in the study. After reviewing several journals regarding this type of research including Scandura and Williams (2000), Gable (1994, April), and Downey and Duane (1979, December), it is apparent that the various techniques that are commonly utilized to include: (a) graphical description that presents graphs to summarize data, (b) tabular description that utilizes tables to summarize data, or (c) summary statistics that calculate definite values to summarize data. These presentations will reveal the measure of central tendency and a measure of statistical variability. Inferential statistics is sometimes utilized by the researcher to make deductive conclusions concerning the unknown aspect of an IT project management population. The researcher can also employ the mathematical statistics which involves probability theory and other various aspects of mathematical components of applied statistics to gain a means of measurement from a purely mathematical standpoint. The data in this aspect often contains some sense of randomness along with a degree of uncertainty. The random phenomena are the premise to provide the researcher a measurable and tangible analysis of quantitative IT project management study.

Qualitative Approach

The actor's methodology is less absolute and more ambiguous than the more quantitative nature of both the analytical and system research methodologies. It assumes the focus is more on the understanding, definition, and action of the subject elements of IT project management subject matters, as the ultimate goal is to create more knowledge in the field. According to Blackler and Brown (1983, July), the downside of this type of qualitative approach is that it has basic tendency of bias information form the actual creator of the knowledge during the actual research procedures employed. In comparison to the other two methodologies that target casual relations and attempt to find an unambiguous result, the actor's methodology seeks to find ambiguity as it is essential in the overall development of IT project management knowledge.

The actor's methodology relies on a more qualitative research approach, which involves a more in depth understanding of the human actions with regard to the subject matter being investigated. This type of qualitative research approach, according to Steenkamp and McCord (2007, Summer), relies on the reasons behind various aspects of human behavior in various IT project management studies. Therefore, qualitative research investigates the why and how of IT project management decisions as opposed to the what, where, and when aspects of a quantitative research study. The research can include ethnography, participant observations, case study analysis, open-ended surveys, and interviews. One could conclude that this type of study is more exploratory instead of specific research, similar to performing a cauterization in the medical field where the doctor is looking for problems (qualitative) versus open-heart by-pass surgery where the doctor is fixing the problem (quantitative). Therefore, the ultimate objective of this research approach is to create knowledge.

Example and Application of Qualitative Approach

In order to create new knowledge, the objective of qualitative research in IT project management studies is to investigate the reasons behind various aspects of behavior but it also can be employed to discover new processes and developments. In reviewing an article by Holmstrom, Fitzgerald, Agerfalk, and Conchuir (2006, Summer), it is apparent that the actor's method utilizing a qualitative approach was employed as the researchers explored how agile software development practices can decrease the three types of distances in global software development, temporal, geographical, and socio-cultural. These researchers included the examination of case studies for precise eXtreme programming and Scrum methodologies used in the software project management process. The research discovered new information regarding these methodologies that is useful in reducing the need for large amount of communication, coordination, and monitoring efforts.

On the other hand, the Lindstrom and Jeffries (2004, Summer) study included an evaluation of various agile methodologies in software development that revealed the underlying values and project team behaviors towards the transition from a traditional software development process to a more agile process. Holmstrom, Fitzgerald, Agerfalk, and Conchuir seemed to concentrate on discovering new approaches and Lindstrom and Jeffries appeared to concentrate on the behavioral aspect. In both cases, the actor's method was deployed in a pure qualitative research study.

Description of Qualitative Process

In qualitative research studies for IT project management studies, the most common data collection techniques revealed in the review of several journals, including Mingers (2001) and Gniewosz (1990, Summer), appears to be the utilization of case studies, ethnography, surveys, interviews, and multiple histories.

A case study in business generally involves an in-depth examination of a single event instead of using large samples with a rigid protocol. This will open the door to tailor the study to discover new IT project management perspectives adding value to the profession as it tends to generate and test hypothesis according to Gummesson (2006). This provides for an organized approach to looking at an event, collecting data, analyzing processed data, and reporting the results. The research might seem systematic in its process but it is still a more unambiguous process as it generates the actual direction during the process.

Kavanagh and Kelly (2002, July) presents the idea of utilizing a sense of ethnography as a perspective that the qualitative researcher utilizing the actor's methodology can create questions and promote action. The general rule is that the researcher will present a description of human social phenomena based on actual work and observations in the fieldwork. In IT project management studies, the researcher will live with the project team to gain first-hand experiences utilizing the business action being studied. The researcher will feel the experiences as a member of the population being studied, the project team, and observe others in the process. Ethnography presents the results as a holistic process as the study will compare positivism and naturalism in terms of their differences and similarities. Since this is a more expensive and time consuming research method, a pure ethnographic process is rarely conducted. Even rare in its utilization, ethnographic methods have sometimes been utilized in the research study of IT project management to obtain first-hand experiences in the actual business settings. The benefit of these type of studies include the discovery of the actual feelings of project team members and project manager that are participating in the common social system of developing new IT projects. For example, one could see how agile development methodologies affect a particular group on a project team by discovering the characteristic attitudes, team member values formed, and behavior patterns. This research method will take a lot of time to accurately arrive at the findings and results in the research study.

Another qualitative research method includes the use of surveys which allows the researcher to examine or look at comprehensively the research question on hand. While surveys are primarily utilized in quantitative studies, it can also be utilized in qualitative studies by using open-ended questions. The qualitative study will most likely utilize interview methods instead of surveys in order to gain an understanding of open ended questions being addressed. In dealing with interview or survey questions, the questions for the qualitative study should be open ended with no pre-specified answers. It is important for the researcher to gather facts, opinions, and speculation. If a face to face interview is conducted, the researcher should observe the body language and emotions. It is important to have a tested interview or survey instrument which is developed by planning in advance, be neutral during the interview or survey process, listen carefully, and always try to seek a diverse view from the participants. Interviews are generally more costly than surveys but will yield the most data to process into information.

The concept of multiple histories in the research of IT project management studies is the idea to reason backwards through a review of historical activities and projects. A researcher would observe through the review of documentation and results of past IT projects in an effort to determine problems or opportunities for improvement with existing processes. The researcher could look for an organizational direction and determine if current processes are aligning the IT strategies to that of the business strategies. Therefore, this is a research approach that studies an issue from tracing backwards from the current situation to look for new approaches that will enhance future IT project management endeavors.

Quantitative Studies Limitations

One limitation to the quantitative study in IT project management research is that it tends to measure existing business theories and practices instead of leading to new discoveries. This type of study requires a researcher's comfort with the rhetorical and methodological assumptions of the quantitative paradigm, along with strong computer statistical skills, technical writing abilities, and library research experience. The psychological characteristic of the quantitative researcher is heavily dependent upon the comfort zone with rules and guidelines while conducting research with a low tolerance towards ambiguity. An individual who uses the brain hemisphere that utilizes reason and rational thought will do well with this type of structure. There must be a body of literature that exists with known variables and existing theories. New theories will not be generated from this type of study and could be the biggest limitation. The changing business environment generally requires the discovery of new theories to adapt to the turbulent environment of IT development.

There are some threats to the internal validity of the research study that includes the occurrence of any event that is not a part of the experiment could have an effect on the dependent variable within the study. The physical and psychological changes of the participation during the research duration could affect the measure of the dependent variable. The actual instrumentation utilized could lead to unreliability, lack of consistency, or create a sense of bias. The survey instrument could be misinterpreted by the participant, for example "where are you from?" could be interpreted as "where were you born," "where are you living now," or "where did you grow up?" The questions could also lead the participant to answer a question differently based on how the question is asked. This could lead the participant to answer a question about how the researcher wants it to be answered, causing unreliability due to biased issues. Also, how the participants are selected could lead to bias as well. There are also some threats to the external validity include the environment where the study is performed depending on the setting, working conditions, and stress levels of the participants. These could also have an effect on the bias outcome on the results.

Issues of Bias and Limitations for Qualitative Studies

There is an issue of bias within the qualitative research especially since the qualitative research relies on the brain hemisphere that depends on creativity. The actor's approach to research is to conduct a study until nothing new could be discovered. A bias could be formed as this research process develops, especially if the researcher has already determined what kind of outcome and mental frame is needed for changes in IT project management techniques. It is easy to lead the discovery to the bias of the researcher or even to that of the research sponsor.

The qualitative research is also limited as it is the start of discovering new aspects of IT project management developments and does not measure tangible success. In other words, the results are not concrete and usually require further study in the future. While the quantitative study is limited to the study of existing IT project management techniques, the qualitative study is limited to finding new discoveries without measurable tangible outcomes.

Mixed Research Methods to Mitigate Limitations and Biases

Steenkamp and McCord (2007, Summer) presents the idea of mixing the business research methods to provide research processes and frameworks combining both qualitative and quantitative research methods for a way to increase the validity and creation of knowledge. In IT project management research studies, the use of mixed approaches aids in the mitigation of limitations and biases that a single design business research would inherit. The degree of triangulation, according to Steenkamp and McCord, can range from a quite simple design to a more complex business research design. Hurmerin-Peltomaki and Nummela (2004) presents that a business researcher utilizing mixed methods should be seeking a research strategy where the utilization of a qualitative method will facilitate the quantitative portion of the study. Some researchers in IT project management research studies will consider this a more complete process but one could consider the utilization of qualitative studies to generate new concepts. Then, the validation of the qualitative study could be completed with the process of a quantitative study in further research initiatives. In essence, the research method choice depends on the actual purpose of the IT project management study.

Conclusion

The significant differences between the quantitative analysis of both analytical and systematic research methods and the qualitative analysis of the actor's research method are that qualitative data involves words and quantitative data involves numbers. Qualitative research is more inductive while quantitative is more deductive in its approach. Qualitative research does not require a hypothesis to begin the research in IT project management studies while the quantitative research must start with a hypothesis. Another significant difference includes the underlying assumptions as the qualitative researcher will learn more about the IT project management situation by either participating or becoming immersed in it, while the quantitative researcher is basically an objective observer as they tend not to participate by using primarily closed-ended surveying instruments.

As the field of IT project management has been advancing to face the needs of a turbulent competitive business world, it has grown harder to align IT strategies with that of the constant changing business strategies. The need for research studies to discover better methods and approaches in an effort to better align these two strategies have become important. There are three primary research methodologies that have been utilized to conduct studies in the IT Project Management arena. These research methods include an analytical approach, systems approach, and actor's approach. Depending on the approach utilized in the study of IT Project Management, either a quantitative, qualitative, or mixed research process will be utilized. Each method has a purpose and process, along with issues of bias and limitations. The research methodologies used are generally dependent upon the paradigmatic assumptions of managing IT projects. The paradigmatic assumptions within the project management business process are the basic truism that build the IT world based on one's experiences, including the messages one receives from significant figures within one's professional path. Once the paradigm is developed, the business research study can begin with these paradigmatic aspects: (1) the stress of one group of events and facts over

another, (2) the attempt to demonstrate agreement between
the paradigm and reality, and (3) the further refinement of the
paradigm.

Speech 5: Model for Improving Agile Development Results (Presentation of Chapter 5 of the Dissertation)

Introduction

Although there was previous research about the definition of agile development and some details of the specific agile methodologies, there did not appear to be any empirical research that addressed the opinions of project managers utilizing these current approaches in software development. The arguments for or against agile software development make sense when taken within the context regarding the benefit of speed, adaptability, and quality of the agile approach but there was no certainty that these three benefits were actually achieved when applied by software development project managers. It was important to see if project managers can see a realization of faster user benefit, an assurance of quality software deployment, and a realization of flexibility to adapt to business changes without affecting quality, schedule, and cost.

This research dealt with the opinions, thoughts, and actual experiences of software project managers working with application software projects that used one of the agile development methodologies. Its purpose was to determine the effectiveness and efficiency of utilizing agile methodologies to ensure rapid deployment in a changing business environment. A survey of the software group within the Project Management Institute (PMI) which included both structured and open-ended items was used to gain some perspective of this growing aspect of application development. Closed-ended questions were included to help keep some sense of statistical control over the data.

Summary of Results

There were 33 respondents, with 27 of the software project managers who actually had experience in managing agile software development projects. It appears that a majority of software project managers using agile approaches used either scrum or extreme programming. The next two approaches that project managers used were feature driven development and rapid application development.

Nineteen project managers with agile software development experience responded to the questions regarding the number of iterations and the length of agile software projects. The average agile project had nine and a half average number of iterations lasting an average of one and one-third months each. Based on the averages from the survey results, it appears that the average agile project lasts for about 11 months. The end-user will see a benefit of the project within the first 40 days of the project as the first iteration is completed, as the average length of an iteration was one month and ten days (1.37 months).

The consensus of the respondents indicated that they felt breaking the project up into smaller components (iterations) aided in the ability to adapt to changes within the business environment. A majority of the respondents felt that uncontrolled changes within the software development project (scope creep) was either reduced or eliminated with use of agile software development processes than with the more traditional software development approaches.

Eighteen project managers responded to the questions relating to project success and quality. In software application development projects, a clear majority indicated that the agile software project was successful in the eyes of the project sponsor and that all the requirements were met according the business users in the projects using agile development methods. Additionally, the majority of the respondents stated that the requirements were implemented in a timely fashion.

A consensus of project managers responding indicated that there were less critical defects found during any testing process during this agile development project that was carried into the production environment. Only 8 of 19 project managers stated that there were a critical or a high level of defects found during the final quality assurance testing process during this agile development project. Of these 8 respondents, 5 stated that there were a critical or a high level of defects found during the final user acceptance testing process in the agile software development project. There seemed to be a consensus that there was an overall user satisfaction for the deployed agile software projects.

Overall, it is apparent that most of these project managers saw success when an agile development approach was used. Success seemed to be more prevalent when users and management support were part of the approach. The use of case tools only served to aid in the project success, especially when it relates to the overall speed of completing the user requirements. Fourteen out of 18 project managers responding indicated that users were involved. Only 7 of the 18 respondents stated that case tools were used.

Discussion of Results

An analysis of the reasons for this belief of success of the agile project by the business sponsor reveals varied responses by project managers. An overall consensus appeared to be that (a) the project experienced more clarification of components and future intent that past projects due to user involvement, (b) the team was easily able to identify additional features that added value to the project cycle and did not incur significant costs, and (c) the testers and developers took more of an active and imaginative role identifying the potential use cases of end users and stakeholders. The teamwork of the participants, user involvement, and experienced developers with a desire to understand the overall business strategy were critical to the project's success. Other respondents also indicated that flexibility, adaptability, and time of delivery expectations being met were important to the business sponsor. The business sponsor seems to consider the project a success when the requested agile project delivers the desired functionality within the time frame expected.

Those project managers not having user involvement had project issues related to project success as related to at least one of the following: (a) timely implementation of requirements, (b) project success with either user or sponsor, and (c) the number of defects. It was noted that 3 out of the 4 project managers reporting lack of user involvement indicated project success according to the business sponsor. However, 2 of these 4 project managers indicated that requirements were not implemented in a timely manner. All four of these respondents reported that the total number of defects were not fewer with this agile development methodology versus the traditional waterfall method.

The project quality at implementation according to a majority of the project sponsors were successful due to the fact that these agile software projects had the following components: (a) much clearer definition of goals at a more granular level, (b) tight coupling of business and technical objectives thorough planning processes along with a close collaboration between business and technology teams, (c) focus on delivering business value, (d) delivering consistent deliverables in short intervals, (e) transparency into the process and progress, and (f) the ability to identifying problems early in the project process.

Summary Statement

Based on the project managers responding to the survey, it appears that the agile development of application software is an effective and efficient development approach to deploy application software while allowing IT projects to be adaptive to a changing business strategy environment. There was an overwhelming consensus among the project managers that agile software development improves adaptability to changing business environment, team communication, team cohesiveness, and team responsiveness to the business needs. Additionally, a reduction in the overall project completion time was reported by a consensus of the project managers.

However, although agile development allows for timely delivery of application software, there were some concerns regarding quality and business user satisfaction. Based on the results, several project managers pointed out issues with system performance. This appeared to be the significant quality related issue noted by the respondents. One project, for example, had a spike of traffic once the system components were implemented. Another project dealt with issues with performance upon implementation as they stated that there was insufficient time for performance design and testing. The

system performance issues were able to be resolved and the
project managers indicated overall success. Several had
suggestions on how to improve future agile software projects.

A consensus of the respondents was that the following ideas
would improve the success of future agile software
development projects: (a) ensuring that all project team
members have been trained in the agile approach used, (b)
guaranteeing that users will be involved in the process, (c)
ensuring that the team includes experience professionals, (d)
improving the steps to ensure performance requirements are
being met during the agile process of each iteration, and (e)
creating a better understanding of the requirements prior to
starting the process. Some respondents stated that
communication is critical to ensure an understanding of the
issues and required tasks. Communication is an important
element to ensuring a better understanding of the
requirements for the project. Additionally, ensuring the users
are involved in the agile process will prevent
miscommunications and confusion of the issues and required
tasks. Although communication is key to ensuring a better
understanding of the business user expectations, their
involvement in the process will help build this important aspect.

Implications for Further Research

Computer Assisted Software Engineering (CASE) tools are
software providing support of the software development
process and were originally created to aid the development of
object oriented programming projects, but can be applied to
basically any type of software development. There needs to be
further study about the correlation of case tools to the

efficiency of completing agile software projects and timeliness of meeting user requirements. The research revealed only 7 out of 18 respondents stated that CASE tools were employed in the agile development project. This means that a majority (11 out of 18) did not employ CASE tools. An interesting aspect of the data received from these project managers is the relationship between implementing requirements in a timely fashion and the use of CASE tools. Four of these 11 respondents who did not use CASE tools reported not meeting the deadlines for implementing requirements. However, the seven of the respondents who used CASE tools reported timely fashion of implementing requirements.

Additionally, 3 of the 11 respondents not using CASE tools reported that the agile development process was not successful according to the business sponsor. Six out of 7 project managers reporting that they use CASE tools stated that the agile development process was successful according to the business sponsor (this is all but one).

Although these are interesting results, it is difficult to determine a correlation between the use of case tools and the efficiency of completing the software development project, including timely completion of user requirements. The survey would need to be expanded or further interview techniques would be needed to derive any such correlations. Another possibility would include a case study observation between two different software projects, one using case tools and another one not using case tools. Therefore, further research in such correlation should be explored in further research.

Implications for Practice and Recommendations

There are several implications that this research has revealed. A software project choosing to use an agile approach to software development should consider several factors. First, the project manager should ensure that all project team members have been trained in the agile approach being used. Prior to starting an agile development project, team members should go through the agile methodology training. Additionally, the team should include experienced team members with the non-experienced members to ensure on the job training which should be in addition to the initial training. Another important aspect is that the project manager should ensure the team includes experienced professionals. The knowledge of the interrelationships of the agile approach through initial training, in conjunction with the first-hand experience of those members who have used the approach in previous projects, will allow the agile project to meet the challenges that introducing a new agile approach to an organization used to traditional methods can bring.

There needs to be an assurance that the business users will be involved in the entire agile process. User involvement is one of the key requirements to making an agile approach successful. It is important to show the business users and sponsors the long-term benefits of giving up the opportunity costs by having experienced users involved. When the user and sponsor realize that the user will see benefits of the software sooner and allow for adaptation to a rapidly changing business environment, there should be an acceptance of the opportunity costs by having users involved. Additionally, quality will be improved with the involvement of business users within the agile development process.

It is important to improve the steps to ensure performance requirements are being met during the agile process of each iteration. Adding an iteration to validate system performance will ensure that system performance issues will be reduced during system implementation. This would appear to be a good approach to ensure system performance. Since the average iteration is about one month and ten days and since it usually takes about a month to resolve system performance issues after implementation based on the respondents, it may be better to consider this approach of spending an iteration to validate performance before actual implementation. However, it is important to note that most project managers felt the critical point regarding quality relating to performance is to ensure that seasoned engineers are involved in the agile projects so that the performance issues are not ignored or overlooked.

It is important to have a better understanding of the requirements prior to starting the process. A key element in starting any project is to have a clear definition of the objective prior to starting the project. Agile software projects are not an exception to the rule. Although the user involvement aids in the development of requirements and allows for adaptation of business environment changes, the overall requirements and purpose needs to be defined prior to starting the process. Starting an agile software project without clearly defining business user requirements is like building a new expressway without the blueprints. Therefore, a clear understanding of the requirements and system objective is important at the starting line. The actual development and adaptation to business changes can be done with the involvement of the business users.

Relationship of Results to Theory

The researchers in a majority of the articles have generally concluded that the delivery of working, tested, and deployable software on an incremental basis will increase value and adaptability much earlier in the lifecycle while significantly reducing the project risk. This is accomplished through dividing the entire software projects into smaller components called iterations. Based on the results from the current research, the project managers indicated that there was an average of nine and a half iterations, with each iteration averaging one month and ten days to complete.

The previous researchers indicated that an agile systems development approach can be used to decrease the time needed to complete the design and quickly deploy application systems (Calvert, 1996). There are two primary advantages to this approach: the increased speed and quality of the applications development process (Valacich et al., 2001). Agile development differs from the more traditional waterfall approach, which most companies favor, in that it is linear and moves in strict order from concept through design, implementation, testing, installation, and troubleshooting, and ends up at operation and maintenance. Agile development is more of a conceptual framework that has been designed to shorten the software development lifecycle with small working packages that are fully functional and can be used to get parts of an application working before the overall project is complete (Valacich et al., 2001). This concept will bring maximum benefits early as agile methods are designed to minimize the risk in software engineering projects by creating small iterations of various components.

Regarding the first assertion of speed of deploying application systems, it is apparent that users do see a benefit quicker. Based on the averages from the survey results, it appears that the average agile project lasts for about 11 months. The end-user will see a benefit of the project within the first 40 days of the project as the first iteration is completed, considering the average length of an iteration was one month and ten days. Several project managers reported that an iteration may be completed as soon as two weeks. The longest an iteration lasted according to one project manager was four months. Based on most research, the waterfall methodology takes a long time to deliver software to production, which typically lasts more than a year. Since the effort involved for the waterfall approach involves the definition of all features of the software project prior to its development and implementation, the user will typically not see any benefit of the new system until at least one year whereas the iteration approach will deliver features to the user typically after the first iteration. Therefore, the speed of users receiving usable components does seem evident with an agile approach.

The researchers in a majority of the articles have generally concluded that the delivery of working, tested, and deployable software on an incremental basis will increase value and adaptability much earlier in the lifecycle while significantly reducing the project risk. Eighteen out of 21 project managers felt that breaking the project up into smaller components aided in the ability to adapt to changes within the business environment. Eleven out of 18 respondents felt that scope creep was either reduced or eliminated while using an agile approach. The flexibility of the agile approach was recognized by a major of project managers. Typically, a waterfall approach has a problem when changes are tried to be incorporated as it generally leads to more confusion and further delays in the project called scope creep. Since a majority of respondents in this research felt that uncontrolled changes within the software development project (scope creep) was either reduced or eliminated with use of an agile software development processes than with the more traditional software development approaches, one can conclude that the agile approach is truly more flexible.

The second primary advantage of an agile development approach according to the researchers is the quality of the applications development process. Even though the need for faster delivery of software development has become evident over the years, quality of computer application systems still is important as they are designed. Improving quality is not just the action of simply meeting user requirements, as it must include the measures of tangible objectives and criteria to demonstrate the software achievement to organizational objectives (Meso & Jain, 2006). Ensuring high quality will require much more than the participation of the testing team: it requires that the entire team, including users, take ownership in system quality and participate in all phases of development over the system life cycle. This is one of the benefits of agile development methodologies as it enables early testing and a continuous approach (Valacich et al., 2001). This agile development of utilizing an iterative development process supporting this continuous testing and improvement process seems to increase the quality of software and is a primary tangible result of agile methodologies (Meso & Jain, 2006).

Overall, most project managers revealed overall project success and quality results, with the possible exception of system performance. Further analysis of the comments made by the project managers revealed that there were issues for these projects with these quality problems, such as users not being fully committed and lack of seasoned engineers in the development team. Both are key elements according to the previous researchers. This data supports the fact that these components are important for a successful agile software development project.

With a majority of the project managers reporting quality software deployments and agile project success, one could conclude that the agile development process does allow for timely delivery of application software while still preserving quality and business user satisfaction, as stated by the previous researchers. However, it is important to ensure total user involvement and seasoned engineers, which appeared to be the issues surrounding the projects with quality problems such as poor system performance. Project managers were concerned that performance standards were not met when completing the agile software project. A suggestion would be for the team to work with the business users and other information technology specialists to ensure that the team will pay more attention to performance requirements. These include user response times, network bandwidth, and ensuring that the system does not waste valuable resources such as memory, disk space, and processor utilization.

Project managers also were concerned that the team has a deeper elaboration on the business user requirements prior to splitting the requirements into increments. This includes the priorities of the requirements. The understanding of requirements will affect the overall quality of the completed project, as well as for each increment. The application system requirements include functionality, usability, and performance.

The research with these project managers revealed some important results regarding agile software development approach not revealed by previous researchers. Adequate training of the agile process to all team members, which includes management and the participating business users, will create a better agile approach framework for the team. It is apparent by the responses that many project managers felt they were thrown into this new agile approach without adequate training. An important element to follow training is the actual practice in a real live project alongside the experienced agile professionals. By having experienced professionals with agile software development experience, adequate coaching on a daily basis will be provided for better on the job training of those with less agile experience. The right resource mix on an agile project team is critical to ensure project success, and agile experience on the team is a requirement to ensure overall success.

Limitations

The survey document used in the data collection process included a field test with the validation of the survey instrument via expert agreement review conducted by the mentor and committee members, as well as being reviewed by the Project

Management Institute (PMI) research committee which had to provide consent prior to using the survey document. A pilot study for survey instruments created from scratch is usually conducted to determine if the proposed survey document will produce the anticipated results.

Since the pilot study would have used valuable resources of respondents with actual software development project management experience within the PMI organization, a pilot test was not conducted prior to the actual data collection process. Since only 27 project managers who had actual agile software development experience had agreed to partake in the study, this was a wise choice. However, this produced a research risk within the survey document at not producing successful research data. The pilot study could have revealed any deficiencies in the survey document design prior to using it on a larger scale research. Therefore, the research was started with the risk that some of the questions may not be usable if the results received by the respondents presented a case that the question was not understood by the project managers as intended.

After reviewing the data, there were only two questions that had any issue. Survey question number three had one issue ("Please estimate the length of time it took to complete each iteration of the project"). The problem noted by some respondents was that the field for the answer did not allow for half a month. However, this did not create a significant issue since those who had iterations that lasted only half a month were able to indicate as such in the comment section of the question, which some of the respondents did.

The second question with an issue was number sixteen ("Were the users involved in the agile development project?"). The question intended to mean that users were fully involved in the entire process but some project managers indicated a positive response but placed in the comment textbox that the users were involved in a more limited capacity. Since most of these project managers indicated the actual involvement within the comments portion of this question, this issue was also mitigated. Therefore, even though not conducting a pilot study was a limitation for this research study, the results did not appear to be affected and the research results were still a success.

Another limitation in this study was the actual small sample size due to the number of respondents within the established time frame of one hundred days (June 11, 2009 through September 18, 2009). A small sample size has a larger risk that the important relationships from the data will not be detected as statistical tests normally necessitate a larger sample size to rationalize and defend that the effect did not happen by chance alone. Although the sample size was small, there were some noteworthy correlations detected especially with regards to the success of the agile software project and user involvement. However, the research data did not present an actual relationship with regards to improving efficiency by using case tools. This only presents an opportunity for future research studies, as already discussed.

Summary and Conclusion

Based on the project managers responding, there were several advantages and disadvantages of the agile software developmental approach reported in the survey results, based on their actual experiences. The key advantages through overwhelming consensus among the project managers were that agile software development improves adaptability to changing business environment, the clearer definition of business goal, team communication, team cohesiveness, and team responsiveness to the business needs. Additionally, a reduction in the overall project completion time was reported by a consensus of the project managers. The improved transparency between the developer and user was a welcomed benefit to the project managers of agile software projects.

The chief disadvantages noted by consensus were the requirement for heavy user involvement, the need for an experienced mature development team, support teams not being in alignment with the agile approach, and a lack of understanding of the agile approach among the business user community. Training costs of team members and business users for organizations more familiar with the traditional waterfall approach is higher when converting to the newer agile approach. Sometimes when a lack of understanding takes place on the project amongst the business user and team members of the agile project, there was a tendency to lead the default back to the conventional waterfall approach. Strong leadership of the project manager was required to prevent this from occurring.

Suggestions made by the respondents that will help improve future agile development projects that they will manage in the future include: (a) ensuring that all project team members have been trained in the agile approach used, (b) guaranteeing that users will be involved in the process, (c) ensuring that the team includes experience professionals, (d) improving the steps to ensure performance requirements are being met during the agile process of each iteration, and (e) creating a better understanding of the requirements prior to starting the process. Some respondents stated that communication is critical to ensure an understanding of the issues and required tasks. Communication is an important element to ensuring a better understanding of the requirements for the project. Additionally, ensuring the users are involved in the agile process will prevent miscommunications and confusion of the issues and required tasks. Although communication is key to ensure a better understanding of the business user expectations, their involvement in the process will help build this important aspect.

The project managers surveyed provided a consensus that agile development of application software can be seen as an effective and efficient methodology to deploy application software while allowing IT projects to be adaptive to a changing business strategy environment. There seems to be a consensus that agile development does allow for timely delivery of application software while still preserving quality and business user satisfaction. For those reporting quality issues, it appeared that the more significant issue dealt with poor system performance after implementation. Further review of comments provided seemed to indicate that lack of user involvement and of seasoned engineers being on the team were contributing factors to these quality issues. Considering user involvement and experienced team members are key elements of an agile approach, this indicates that the agile approach will preserve quality as long as all key components are in place.

Speech 6: The History of Computers and the Internet

The purpose of this presentation is to discuss the history of computers and the internet, along the future of the internet. We will start with the discussion of computers in general.

The History of Computers

The first actual event dealing with computers was in 1939 when Bill Hewlett and David Packard created the first known computer in their garage. The HP 200A Audio Oscillator was developed and utilized by engineers as testing equipment. Walt Disney Pictures used an upgraded version of this in the movie "Fantasia" as sound effect generators. The birth of Hewlett-Packard was formed. The Complex Number Calculator was created and developed by George Stibitz in 1940. This equipment used telephone lines for a Teletype connection in order to perform mathematical calculations at a remote site. This is the birth of remote access computing. Between 1939 and 1942, a college professor, John Atanasoff, and a graduate student, Cliff Berry, produced the Atanasoff-Berry Computer. This was the ground work of basic computer principals but its patent was challenged by John Mauchly who co-designed the Electronic Numerical Integrator and Computer (ENIAC). It was resolved in 1973 as it was evident that John Mauchly examined the other computer before creating the ENAIC. The end result of the legal claim declared Atanasoff as the originator of many simple computer ideas but the concept of computers was declared un-patentable. A project visualized by Harvard professor Howard Aiken was stared. The end result was a computer designed and manufactured by IBM, the Harvard Mark-1. It was basically a relay-based calculator.

During World War II, John Mauchy and John Presper Eckert who were part of the University of Pennsylvania were contracted to form a project team by the U.S. Army. As a result, the ENAIC was formed as they developed a modular computer that could compute addition and subtraction functions, as well as holding a ten-digit number within its internal memory. The concept was aided after John Mauchy examined the Atanasoff-Berry Computer first, even though this computer expanded computing even further. During the same time, a project team from the Massachusetts Institute of Technology was contracted by the U.S. Navy to build a bomber crew simulator in order to train new crews. As a result, the project team planned to build a substantially large analog computer but made a decision to construct a digital computer after reviewing and examining the ENIAC computer. In 1951, the Navy lost interest in the project and it was picked up by the Air Force which would design the Semi-Automatic Ground Environment (SAGE) program.

In the 1950's, the Universal Automatic Computer (UNIVAC) was manufactured by Remington Rand (now Unisys) and was delivered to the U.S. Census Bureau. John Mauchy and John Presper Eckert were the lead on this project for Remington Rand. This became the first commercial computer to draw extensive public attention. Some people called this first commercial computer the "IBM UNIVAC" but this is not part of IBM. Remington Rand ultimately sold 46 of these computers at more than one million dollars for each computer. Remington Rand became Sperry-Rand, and finally Unisys. IBM was not the first commercial computer produced as many may think, but instead Remington Rand was the first manufacturer to develop a commercial computer. CBS News borrowed a UNIVAC on

November 4, 1952, in order to predict the outcome of the presidential race. All of the opinion polls pointed to Stevenson as winning the election; however, the UNIVAC helped Walter Cronkite to forecast Eisenhower as the winner, even though they waited until very late to proclaim and announce the UNIVAC's actual prediction.

IBM created the IBM701 EDPM Computer in the 1950's to become the second commercial computer, after the UNIVAC. However, this computer was a general purpose computing machine and was originally used as a defense calculator for the Korean War. Only nineteen of these computers from IBM were manufactured and the computer rented for $15,000 per month. A new computer in 1955 was created by AT&T Bell Laboratories proclaimed the first fully transistorized computer, TRADIC. It included nearly 800 transistors as opposed to vacuum tubes that the previous computers utilized. The transistors were cold, highly efficient amplifying devices developed at the Bell Labs and allowed the computer to run on less than 100 watts, which is one-twentieth the energy that was necessary by means of the vacuum tube computers. In the 1960's, IBM commercialized these transistor computers. The computer age up to this point was known as the computing stage since the first functions of the computers were used as an aid in calculating numbers.

In 1955, the Electronic Recording Method of Accounting (ERMA) was developed for the banking industry by the Stanford Research Institute. It started as a project for Bank of America in an attempt to computerize and automate processes within the banking industry. This project computerized the former manual processing of checks, account management, and updating of demand deposit accounts. The magnetic ink character recognition (MICR) program was invented by Stanford as part of

the ERMA and allowed the computers to read the numbers at
the bottom of a check that were a special font in order to
automatically track and account for demand deposit
transactions. The ERMA and MICR inventions were tested on
real bank accounts at the end of 1956. General Electric
produced the actual models purchased and implanted by Bank
of America in 1959 as the bank's accounting and check handling
computerized system. These computers were utilized in the
banking industry until the 1970's.

Along with the banking industry, many other financial
institutions such as thrifts, insurance companies, and such were
automating their processes with computers during the 1960's
and 1970's. The expansion of computers in other industries
occurred during the late 1970's and 1980's. The computers
were basically either large mainframes or midrange
computerized platforms. The chief business process benefiting
from the computerization of business processes was the
Accounting and Finance divisions within an organization. The
other divisions only received side benefits as the applications
developed on these computers were primarily financial and
accounting orientated. As a matter of fact, most computer
departments reported to the Chief Financial Officer or
Accounting Director during this growth in the deployments of
computers. As the computers expanded in the business
environment in the 1960's and 1970's, the computer
departments were called Electronic Data Processing (EDP) and
the applications were tied to a few accounting functions:
general ledger, payables, receivables, payroll, inventory, billing,
and cash management.

The programming in business was primarily written in Common Business-Oriented Language (COBOL). Grace Hopper, who was a mathematician and computer scientist in the Navy, developed a compiling program in 1952 that permitted a computer programmer to use English-like words instead of numbers. This was called the Bomarc system and eventually would lead to the development of COBOL in 1959 and was utilized by the UNIVAC computer developed by Remington Rand, where Grace Hopper worked after leaving the Navy.

During the end of the 1970's, During this time frame, Robert Metcalfe invented Ethernet in order to allow fast data transfer by linking several computers within the same location using hardware running from workstation to workstation. This invention took over three years to perfect so that this network would be fast enough to link hundreds of computers and peripherals within the same location or building. Prior to this invention, no more than two or three computers could be connected at any one location. This would ultimately lead to the final stage of the data processing era.

In the 1980's, local area networks and personal computers were being installed for selected functions within the business environment. As existing functions within various departments set up with their own computer systems, the end-user tasks become easier and less dependent upon the data processing department, especially with Word Processing and Spreadsheet software becoming available. The main focus at this time was to automate existing business processes in an effort to create better efficiencies.

During the end of the 1980's and the beginning of the 1990's, the Information Systems stage emerged. The corporate standard was the creation of wide area networks. There was a movement in the use other programming languages such as Visual Basic, Java, HTML, C++, etc., leading to a movement to relational database management systems. Senior management began looking for ways to migrate towards system and data integration, eliminating the stand-alone systems. Additionally, there was a concentration on processing data to become useful information for management to make decisions. The main focus was based on central control and corporate learning as senior management found the computer age useful towards improving their job functions, as well as all managers through the corporate chain of command. The Information Systems department started more concentration on network support, system integration, and database administration. As a result, there was a movement in several organizations to create a Chief Information Officer (CIO) with a reporting responsibility to a Senior Management Committee or even the President, instead of the Accounting or Finance directors.

During the end of the 1990's and beginning of 2000, the wide area networks expanded via the Internet. These networks concentrated on the inclusion of global enterprise systems and various business processes to improve supply chain and distribution activities. Senior management expanded their desire to improve the sharing of data across all systems as system integration was the goal. The main focus in the end of the information systems stage was to improve the efficiencies and speed in manufacturing, inventory control, and distribution. At the end of this stage, marketing departments were processing data into useful information for revenue enhancement and marketing techniques. This was done by improving data mining techniques to find useful relationships of data that can be used to improve the targeting of marketing segments and opportunities. The Internet has generated new promotional and marketing activities that have enhanced the overall value to the information systems stage.

As the business environment moved into the twenty-first century and the improved of operational efficiencies became the objective of technology, the movement into the information technology stage emerges. A lot of organizations changed the name of the Chief Information Officer (CIO) to Chief Technology Officer (CTO). This is where organizations added hand-held devices, remote processing, and the use of cell phone technologies as a method to improve accounting (mostly payment processing), operations (inventory control and supply chain management), and marketing. The Internet has also changed the way a lot of individuals conduct business and businesses have found a need to take advantages of these new technology opportunities.

Electronic commerce (E-Commerce) has become a new method of conducting business especially in the banking, retail, entertainment, education, and governmental services areas. The use of technology has moved in all aspects of business activities including business-to-business (B2B), business-to-consumer (B2B), consumer-to-consumer (C2C), business-to-government (B2G), consumer-to-government (C2G), government-to-government (G2G), government-to-employee (G2E), and business-to-employee (B2E). This includes supply chain activities, retailing, information distribution, marketing, and even the payment of taxes and fines. The overall economy has now become dependent on information technology.

History of the Internet

The history of the internet started with President Eisenhower in 1958 when he signed the funding for the Advanced Research Projects Agency Network (ARPAnet) within the U. S. Air Force appropriations bill. This set the stage for the development of the technology that ultimately leads to the internet being utilized currently. Under this funding allocation there were two scientists in 1962, J. C. R. Licklider and W. Clark that authored *"One Line Man Computer Communications"* which was the first internet concept paper. In 1965, Len Kleinrock authored a paper entitled, *"Communications Net"* which describes the design for a packet switching network utilized for ARPAnet.

Robert Taylor, the head of the Defense Advanced Research Projects Agency in 1969, decided to use Licklider's concept and assign Kleinrock to initiate a project to build such a network, where the initial connection was established between two research institutes, University of California in Los Angeles and Stanford Research Institute that same year. Later in the same year, Kleinrock added University of Utah and University of California in Santa Barbara. This created a 4-node network and an internet revolution was in its grassroots. Over an eleven year period, the number of hosts had expanded past 200 locations across the ARPAnet in order for it to become a technical hub and foundation for today's internet. By 1984, the number of hosts reaches 1000. The results of this development led to the creation of internet technologies currently utilized in businesses, including both intranet and extranet.

Electronic mail (e-mail) is a network capable email system that was first developed for the ARPAnet project. This message exchange system was created by Ray Tomlinson in 1972 by developing two email programs called SNDMSG and READMAIL. Files were copied over the network within this email system. Tomlison's first concern was to create an addressing method that would be meaningful. He thought of using the notation of "username@hostname" which is the same standard that is utilized today. He decided to use the commercial "at" symbol (@) that combined the user and host names because he felt that there was a natural meaning to those using this messaging system. While these programs were a quite simple design that was driven by using a command line, it established a foundation that still defines the underlying technology that gets one email from one person's location to another party's electronic mailbox.

Vinton Cerf and Robert Kahn designed the Internet network protocol through the ARPAnet project. The TCP/IP communications standard was formed, which classifies data transfer on the Internet currently. This combines the Transmission Control Protocol (TCP) and the Internet Protocol (IP). TCP incorporates both the connection-oriented links and datagram services between hosts. IP is the protocol layer accountable for steering datagram packets across network perimeters. Every computer is assigned a unique address called IP address which defines how the unique information will be utilized to route the data packets from one server or desktop to another server or desktop from anywhere in the world. This evolved into local area networks and the Internet as a standard for commercial utilization in the 1980's. Eventually, the World Wide Web for both commercial and non-commercial use was developed in the early 1990's.

In 1988, the first commercial email system was created by
Vinton Cerf by using a connection of MCI Mail to the National
Science Foundation Network through the Corporation for the
National Research Initiate. This was an experimental use of the
email system which was the first authorized commercial
employment of the Internet. In 1989, Compuserve connected to
the National Science Foundation Network though the Ohio State
University network. In 1993, Delphi and America Online began
to connect their email systems to the Internet which was the
first start of a large adaptation to the globalized accepted
standard of the World Wide Web.

The first connection to the Internet was through a dial up
connection via the telephone lines. In the 1990's, this dial up
connection allowed residential customers to connect to the
Internet which aided in the growth of Internet popularity.
However, there were two disadvantages that became evident:
(a) a dedicated phone line was needed to connect to the
Internet and (b) it was extremely slow. If Ethernet was available
to increase speed within the same location for an organization,
there must be an answer to increase the speed for residential
consumers to gain fast access to the Internet. In the 2000's,
broadband was developed and grew exponentially. It was slow
to take off due to the high cost of this type of Internet Service
Providers but as the competition grew, it eventually caused
prices to drop. Currently, the broadband connection is the norm
for accessing the Internet and the World Wide Web.

The Future of the Internet

We have started using the Internet with our smart phones and
tablets. This has given many individuals access to any

information at any given time. As we can see, the internet has virtually everything available. We will soon in the future see a touch screen integrated into many devices including our cars, refrigerator, table tops, counters, restaurant tables, bathroom stalls, and other such locations. This will create many more opportunities and challenges for interfacing with information on the internet. Cloud computing is also another tool that we are using now and will grow even more in the future. The cloud will be hosting many of our pictures, videos, documents, and such. These can be shared or protected. Webcam has moved to improve communication with such tools as Skype and will continue to grow.

The internet as a medium has evolved at a great speed and will continue to grow causing ever more cultural changes. Print media has been affected as many individuals obtain the news online. Digital medium will continue to grow. We can expect television and movies to be directed via the internet as cable and dish television will eventually die. What we will see in ten years will be miles apart from what we see today. If you have not embraced the internet yet, it is about time to join the bandwagon. The internet will be fully integrated our lives soon and there will be no escape. In this case, it is better to join the movement or be left behind.

Speech 7: IT Competencies for Systems Analysts

Introduction

Most organizations have moved dependent on information systems that are utilized for operational, tactical, and strategic advantage. In order for information

systems to remain effective, these systems must efficiently capture, store, process, and distribute information according to business objectives, which is why systems analyst are important the system development life cycle. Systems analysts are the individuals responsible and accountable for the performance of the systems analysis and design of new and modified systems. Information systems analysis and design must be based on a deep understanding of the organization's objectives, structure, and processes, as well as the analyst's knowledge of how to exploit information technology for competitive advantage. There are some differences between the problem solving competencies that is utilized by the novice and the expert systems analyst. Schenk, Vitalari, & Davis (1998) appear to discuss only two of the competencies that were mentioned by Glen (2003). Glen discusses technical competence (identified also by Schenk), personal productivity, multitasking capability, ability to describe the business context of technical work, ability to forge compromises between business and technical constraints, manageability of client relationships, ability to manage technical teams, play positive politics, expansion of client relationships, make others more productive, manage ambiguity (identified also by Schenk), and time management skills.

Technical Expertise

Shenk et al. (1998) describes technical competence as the ability to have knowledge of specific domains as the experts demonstrated a deeper breadth of domain knowledge than novices as the experts felt comfortable to verbalize more domain specific issues than novices. Expert systems analysts seemed to maintain interest in user issues throughout the task while novices expressed interest only in the early stages. Glen (2003) defines technical competence into two specific parts: technical breadth of general technical knowledge and technical depth of knowledge about a particular technical subject matter. Some may have a narrow breadth of knowledge while others maybe wider. The extensiveness of knowledge is varied by different experience levels. If a systems analyst has experience with COBOL code but not visual basic, java, or other such program code, the breadth of knowledge is narrow and may have trouble with how to design multi-tiered client server application that may involve several different types of technologies. While the breadth discusses the span of general knowledge, the depth of specific area of knowledge will indicate how well the analyst can navigate the structures within a small range of technologies, according to Glen (p. 77).

Shenk et al. indicates that experts will verbalize domain specific issues more than novices while the novices will verbalize user involvement more. The experts will use the bottom up approach in the their problem solving techniques as they tend to focus on a particular business need, while the novice will utilize a more top down approach as they tend to reflect the broader needs of the organization. The expert tend to have a strong focus according to the article in solving requirements by starting with the clerks in a bottom up approach to problem solving because they already have the understanding of the problems deep structures and are looking for the most efficient method to resolving the problem on hand. The novice will focus on determining management needs and employing a more top down approach because do not have the knowledge structure from prior experiences. The top down approach is considered to be weak without employing an overall model of the problem structure. The authors indicate that the evidence supports that by the experts already have a deep understanding of the problem, they are able to look at the most efficient and effective method to present an internal representation of the problem.

Managing Ambiguity

As technical work tend to involve chaos and a lot of confusion, one could say that technical projects involve work that has a lot of ambiguity, regardless how clear it appears on the surface of the project. According to Glen, ambiguity arises because most technological projects (a) are highly complex and fragile constructions, (b) are work in progress, and (c) are requiring the involvement of human beings that contribute to whim and uncertainty (p. 91).

Shenk et al. describes goal setting for problem solving is critical to systems analyst. Goal setting appears to provide a sense of direction for experts in the efforts of subsequent problem solving activities. This goal setting activity is important for the systems analyst to deal with the abstract nature of analyzing problems. The research by the authors reveals that novices tend to verbalize more strategies for solutions than experts. On the other hand, the expert system analysts tend to be more precise about what issues must be resolved for a project to become successful. The authors stated that the experts often indicated a more skeptical tone in their approach than those of novices (p. 32). By using a top down approach, the expert analyst can become more precise about the exact issues that must be resolved for a successful project.

Conclusion

The authors indicate that organizations are becoming more dependent on information systems technology which requires the effectiveness of systems analyst is more important in today's business environment. These specific differences between the novice and expert should be examined in an effort to strengthen the skills of the novice systems analyst. The improvement of these skills will help make information systems to remain effective as these systems must become more efficient in order to capture, store, process, and distribute information in accordance to the pre-defined business objectives. However, based on my personal experiences, a systems analyst needs to have analytical, technical, managerial, and interpersonal skills in order to be successful. Glen seemed to address these skills in his twelve competencies, while Shenk et al. touched only on the technical and analytical skills of systems analyst. The Shenk et al. study provided that novices verbalized a higher frequency of strategies in their problem solving behaviors but verbalized fewer goal, test hypothesis, and discard behaviors. Also, the novice seems to work on a problem at a more general level.

A significant distinction involves the analyst's knowledge base as the novice is characterized by their focus on systems development activities and systems components, and less on function requirements, system procedures, and organizational issues than the more experienced analysts. Experts demonstrated higher level of technical knowledge by the course of their actions and approaches to solving problems than their novice counterparts. The experts also had higher levels of competency in their ability to manage ambiguity by their utilization of several types of methods to obtain a solution to the problem. Ultimately, the systems analyst should have a deeper understanding of the organization's objectives, structure, and processes, along with the knowledge of how to exploit the information technology for creating comparative advantage. The experts have the skills to accomplish this aspect of systems analyst work.

Human Resources and Motivation

These are speeches relating to human resource issues and methods to motivate others.

Speech 1: Two Areas of Concern: ADA and FLSA—Prevent Being Burned

There are two areas in human resources that can be of significant concern: ADA and FLSA. I will explain the reason to be concerned and how to prevent issues for your organization.

The American with Disabilities Act (ADA) was signed into law by George H. W. Bush in 1992 and the ADA Amendment Act (ADAAA) was signed into law by his son, George W. Bush, in 2008 in order to clarify and broaden the definition of disability and the coverage (Bennett-Alexander, 2009). Since the law applies to all employers with 15 or more workers, the company would be required to comply. The claims of obesity were generally rejected by the courts under the original ADA law until the implementation of the ADAAA (Gregg, n.d.). The Equal Employment Opportunity Commission (EEOC) has recognized even basic obesity as a disability since it does have an impact on the individual and their ability to perform various activities in life, such as bending.

A human resource administrator should consider the recent modifications to the definition of the term "disability" and the expansion of the protections of the original ADA that has been granted under the ADAAA. The human resource department should tell management that the determination of any impairment should be made without requiring the knowledge of medications. The simple fact that an employee has a condition that limits their life's functions should be sufficient. The company should not engage in broad investigation and examination to determine if a condition constitutes as a disability. Instead, the human resource department should encourage management to follow the requirement to provide reasonable accommodations to the employees qualified to perform a job with such accommodations.

The human resource department should consider removing any extreme details in the ADA policy as to what constitutes a disability since the definition was expanded to include any condition that limits one to the ability to perform life's basic functions such as bending, breathing, walking, and other such functions. Reasonable accommodations should be made to satisfy the disability claim including obesity. A formalized process should be drafted to ensure the employees can file for reasonable accommodations and how the company can address and review such claims without immediately refusing the request. All managers should consult with the human resource department when there is a question about the validity of a claim. In the review of a valid claim such as an obesity issue, the job description should be scrutinized to ensure that the components in question are truly essential job-related functions that are consistent with a bono fide business necessity.

The ADAAA now defines a disability as any condition meeting one of these three requirements: (a) a physical or mental challenge that limits one or more major life activities or a record of a physical or mental challenge that significantly limits a major life activity (EEOC website). This should be included in a training session to the managers at the company. The company should document the non-discriminatory action taken when an adverse action results in an employee termination for not meeting job requirements or the accommodation is not made to respond to an employee claim. This documentation will reflect due diligence on the behalf of the employer.

Another issue that many human resource departments have to worry about is dealing with the Fair Labor Standards Act (FLSA) which is the groundwork for the U.S. wage laws that created the 40 hour work week, determines overtime pay, minimum wage, and who is eligible for it (Bennett-Alexander, 2009). The FLSA law requires compensation for any non-exempt employee's attendance at meetings, lectures, training programs, and such unless each of the following criteria are met: (a) it is outside the regular working hours, (b) participation is voluntary, (c) employee does not perform any productive work during participation, and (d) this type of activity is not directly related to the employee's job (U.S. Department of Labor, n.d.).

It should be noted that a company is not obligated to pay for time spent as long as he is waiting to be engaged which means the employee needs to be reachable to report to work if needed, while an employee who is engaged to wait, meaning that the employee must stay at the workplace or very near the workplace, is required to be compensated under the FLSA law (Free Legal Advice Website, n.d.).

An employer can perform five items to ensure compliance with FLSA and avoid associated claims. First, the employer should ensure that the job classifications are correct. One of the most common problems regarding FLSA violations is the inappropriate classification of jobs being exempt or non-exempt as everyone can be non-exempt but only certain jobs can be classified as exempt (Bennett-Alexander, 2009). The exempt employee must pass three tests which include a salary test (how much they are paid), the salary basis test (how they are paid), and the duties test (what kind of work they perform). The claims resulting from unpaid overtime can be reduced by classifying the job correctly.

The most common area of FLSA complaints result from the lack of appropriate overtime payment (Bennett-Alexander, 2009). The employer should make sure that the employee time recordkeeping procedures are accurate. Some employers use an electronic time clock to help ensure accuracy. This is important for non-exempt employees as they should always record their starting and ending times accurately, whether it is electronic or manual. The electronic versions are more accurate if it is not too cost prohibitive. As a result of the hours performed, the employer must ensure they pay the employee any required overtime pay they have earned at a rate the wage times 1.5 times the number of hours worked over forty. This is the minimum standard under the FLSA.

A third item that could be implemented to reduce or prevent claims is the periodic review of the human resource manual. This would ensure that it is complete and in compliance with the most current laws. The description of exempt and non-exempt jobs should be a part of the manual. A procedure to follow if an employee feels there is an error or their rights have been violated regarding compensation should be included in the manual, as well.

A fourth item that could be implemented is proper training to supervisors and managers regarding the employer's policies, the FLSA laws, and their duties regarding compliance. This training should be on a periodic basis and prescribe penalties to those supervisors and managers who do not comply. The training procedure will also help in productivity with a motivated workforce as the individuals will have the proper knowledge as to the rules for managing the subordinate employees. Additionally, the employees involved should be advised as to the policy and laws that affect their job.

The fifth item that could be implemented is to document the expectations of certain workers that may have to be on call and those who may volunteer to have additional training outside the work area. The on call employee could be required to carry an employer-issued pager and require the employee to report to work within a reasonable time frame, such as two hours. The employee should never be required to wait at the job location but allowed to perform whatever activities they choose, with the mindset that they may have to report to an emergency requirement. The definition of required training which will be paid for and the type of training that would not be covered. Generally, any training that is outside the normal working hours, voluntary, without any productive work being performed, and is not directly related to the job should be considered as non-paid training. These definitions should be clear, concise, and easy to understand, while being compliant with the FLSA laws.

Speech 2: Avoiding Liability for Potential Title VII Violations

This is a presentation about Title VII as it pertains to disparate impact and disparate treatment policies that should be implemented to avoid liability for potential Title VII violations. I will specifically cover the following areas:

1. The difference between a disparate impact and a disparate treatment claim
2. The complaint procedure for a disparate impact and a disparate treatment claim as it pertains to the EEOC
3. The defenses available to the company should a disparate impact claim and/or a disparate treatment claim be lodged against an organization
4. Suggestions for avoiding potential EEOC claims and complaints

 Title VII of the Civil Rights Act of 1964 protects "minorities, women, and white males over 40, now constitute over 70 percent of the total workforce" (Bennett-Alexander). The law prohibits employers from discriminating covered employees on the bases of race, gender, religion, or national origin. The Equal Employment Opportunity Commission (EEOC) as a part of enforcing the provisions of Title VII will investigate claims, mediate the conflict, and may even file lawsuits on behalf of the covered employees. As a result of this

title, there are two discriminatory actions that employers need to be aware of: (a) disparate treatment theory and (b) disparate impact theory.

The United States courts have defined disparate treatment as discrimination that "the employer simply treats some people less favorably than others because of their race, color, religion, sex, or national origin" (Carper, McKinsey, & West, 2007). Treating one employee in a more favorable fashion due to one's race, gender, religion, or national origin is be a violation of Title VII. Basically, one employee is treated differently from other individuals in the work force in the same work related situation. Let us assume that an organization has a policy of not drinking alcoholic beverages during working hours including lunch breaks. Then, we will further assume that a male employee and female employee have beer at lunch during working hours and the employer fires the female and not the male. If the reason for the different treatment was due to gender, then this would be disparate treatment of gender as it violates Title VII. If the reason for the difference treatment was due to the fact that the female employee had violated the policy several times and it was the male employee's first offense and warning, then this would be disparate treatment because of differences in violation occurrences and would be legal in the spirit of the law. In summary, disparate treatment focuses on the discriminatory intent and proof of discriminatory motive is required.

On the other hand, disparate impact focuses on the actual consequences of the discriminatory actions. This is a theory that would involve the organization giving fair treatment of different groups on the surface (facially neutral) but actually fall more harshly on one group of employees over another which cannot be justified by business need (Bennett-Alexander, 2009). An individual does not have to prove a discriminatory motive under the disparate impact theory (Carper, McKinsey, & West, 2007). Let us assume that the hiring of a cook requires the potential employee to take an intelligence test that does not have a business justification as it relates to the duties of the position. Further, this type of intelligence test statistically has a significant impact on one group over another and screens out vastly more of one group than the other. Then, the organization would be seen as violating Title VII under the disparate impact theory, even though there was not intentional discrimination. This theory can be generally utilized whenever there is a big enough impact based on sex, age, religion, race, or national origin.

The comparison of the two theories is as follows:

- Disparate treatment is the treating of employees differently based on sex, age, religion, race, or national origin; while disparate impact is the result is different based on sex, age, religion, race, or national origin.

- Disparate treatment is actions of the employer are different between the two groups in the same work related situation; while disparate impact is employer practices based on the matter of statistical origin.

- Disparate treatment must prove intent; while disparate impact does not need to prove intent.

The complaint procedure for a disparate impact and a disparate treatment claim calls for local agencies to screen the employee assertions which try to dispose of the case. Generally, the local agencies will require the covered employee to file a claim in person or by mail. However, if the claim cannot be disposed at this level, then the EEOC will investigate the claim and if a violation is apparent, then the agency will try to mediate the conflict between the employer and covered employee (Bennett-Alexander). If necessary, the EEOC will file a lawsuit on behalf of the employee.

The employee would need to prove in a disparate treatment case that the employer treated an individual differently than other employees of another group for the same work related situation and the discrimination was based on color, age, race, disability, national origin, religion, or sex. If the employee was successful in this endeavor, then the employer can provide a defense that the action was for a bona fide occupational qualification. In other words, the employer can prove there were legitimate reasons for the action taken. The employer would defend themselves for this workplace decision, although discriminatory, is rationally and convincingly necessary to the normal operation of that particular business. An example would be the case of Chinese restaurants hiring only Chinese table servers to create a certain atmosphere. This defense is a tremendously thin exception to prohibiting discrimination that can only be invoked when the spirit or the fundamental nature of business operation would be damaged.

The employee would need to prove in a disparate intent case that a neutral employment practice has an unfavorable and adverse consequence on a covered employee group (race, gender, religion). If the employee was successful in this proof, the employer can defend the action by proving the employment practice has a business necessity and it is related to the job. However, if the employee can show that there is a less restrictive alternate practice available to the employer, then the employer will lose the case.

The company should develop concise, written employment policies dealing with human resource matters that include job descriptions, interview and screening procedures, employee handbook, employee disciplinary actions, and employee applications. The employer should ensure that all employee-related actions are documented including terminations. The employer should conduct employee performance reviews that are objective and straightforward. Also, the employer should promptly investigate all allegations of discrimination and harassment that has been reported that should be thorough and seek advice of an employment law counsel before taking action. Employees should be trained on how to report issues without worry of repercussions.

A company might consider starting a six to twelve month project that will involve reviewing and updating the employee handbook, job descriptions, management policies, and human resource procedures. The project will begin with the review the handbook policies, job descriptions, interview and employee screening procedures, and investigation process of handling employee allegations. If any of these are either non-existent, incomplete, or have the potential to create a liability issue for the company, then they should re-write the document so that it will reduce or mitigate the potential of employee complaints of disparate treatment or disparate impact discrimination issues. For example, if a job description has a requirement that could be discriminatory by disparate impact and it is not necessary for the business, then it would be changed to ensure compliancy. At the end of the project, the legal counsel will review the various human resource documents to validate the compliancy requirements.

In conclusion, a disparate impact is unplanned, whereas a disparate treatment is a deliberate action or decision to treat people differently based on race, gender, religion, or national origin. Title VII of the Civil Rights Act of 1964 protects these covered individuals from this type of discriminatory actions in the employment environment. The Equal Employment Opportunity Commission (EEOC) as a part of enforcing the provisions of Title VII will investigate claims, mediate the conflict, and may even file lawsuits on behalf of the covered employees. Starting the project that I suggested in the previous slide will help reduce the potential risk of having these complaints filed against the company.

Speech 3: Role of Paradigms

Organizations have objectives that should be achieved. An organization is an actual structured system where members interact in an effort to obtain these objectives. Having an understanding of organizational paradigms will enhance one's understanding of complex organizations.

It is important to utilize the use of organizational paradigms in order to understand the nature of complex organizations. This is critical as we consider that today's businesses are becoming more complex. Complexity is evident in that many organizations change over time based on my experience of working with several organizations. As businesses become more complex, many decisions have to be made at the higher levels within the organization. At this one organization, several decisions within the information systems group appeared to have a significant effect on overall strategy. Every project had to add organizational value by either saving costs or increasing revenue. If mistakes were made, consequences would occur to the employee making the decision. Therefore, a majority of decisions were pushed up the ladder. Additionally, as one organization expanded these operations after taking over several other organizations within their industry and as they expanded the marketplace to include Europe and Asia. These changes have overwhelmed organizational members with complex problems to create resolutions for. This overwhelming stimulus has led to members over simplifying the most complex solutions. It would lead one to believe that sophisticated guidance is necessary in order to cope. This guidance will start by developing an understanding of complex organizations.

Organizations are the means by which collective goals are accomplished and the needs of society are met. The science of understanding the nature of organizations starts with the idea of understanding the different paradigms of what defines organizations. According to Kuhn (1996), the absence of a paradigm, all the facts that would pertain to the development of a given science may likely seem relevant (p. 15). Kuhn further states that a paradigm is rarely an object for replication (p. 23). Therefore, one should define organization through an understanding of the various paradigms within the systems theory.

When one considers the system theory, one is led to think of the problems with relationships, structures, and interdependence, instead of their constant attributes (Katz and Kahn, 1966). There are three main perspectives of organizations, which are a rational system, a natural system, and an open system. The rational system and natural system appear to view the organization as a closed system. The open system theory is dependent on the environment. It is important to understand these perspectives in order to view the changes of organizational structure. These structural changes are enhanced with the use of paradigms as a lens by which a study will occur as the relationships of the organization restructure, according to Kuhn (1996). This author continues to state that the transformations of the paradigms of physical optics are revolutions and the successive transition from one paradigm to another via revolution is the usual development of mature science (p. 12).

As stated before, it is important to utilize the use of organizational paradigms in order to understand the nature of complex organizations. Organizations are the means by which collective goals are accomplished and the needs of society are met. Organizations generally need the vision of creating opportunities and have the responsibility to bring the resources together to accomplish the collective goals. To truly gain a full understanding of the importance that organizations play in the lives of individuals, it is imperative to study the differing perspectives of organizational systems.

In a rational system perspective, the accomplishment of specific objectives is an important characteristic of an organization, along with the following of written rules and formal roles set to accomplish the specific organizational objective. However, natural systems are collectives that has its members pursue multiple interests but recognize the value of perpetuating the organization, according to Scott (2003, p. 26). Scott argues that the behaviors of the members within the organization is not necessarily guided by the formal roles and written rules, but their own interests guide the behavior of its members. The third perspective of an organization is what Scott (2003) calls an open system. Scott continues to state that it is a system of interdependent activities linking the members, where the systems are embedded in the dependence on continuing exchanges within the environment in which they operate (p. 28). This implies that the environment has an effect on the organization and there is a definite connection of the members within the organization and the environment that surrounds the members.

In formal organizations, the rules of an organization are expected to be followed by the members in order for the

organizational objectives to be
achieved. While this assumes
a closed system, one cannot
forget the interaction
activities of each individual
which implies a need to
understand open systems.
One must consider that an
organization is a structured

process where the organizational members all interact in order
to achieve both individual and organizational objectives. There
are cases that even the most formalized organization must
move away from the formalized rules in order to achieve their
objectives. For example, we should consider the Black Team at
IBM. According to Romero (2002, December 11), a system filled
with defects in the 1960's was considered a defective product
that customers do want to buy. IBM had several defective
systems that cost IBM an excessive amount of money. IBM was
known as a formal organization where the employees had to
wear white shirts, black or grey ties, and coordinated pants. All
employees had to follow specific rules in order to be a member
of their organization. Definitely, IBM was following a rational
system perspective.

Romero (2002, December 11) continues to state that IBM had
lifted their formalized rules in order to implement a testing
team that would help resolve these defect issues in the
software. The Black Team was implemented in order to find
software defects. In order to allow for increased creativity, the
team was allowed to wear all black clothes to generate an
image of villainous destroyers. As a result, the team became

successful in finding defects and programmers feared the Black Team. Romero continues to state that this group was made of slightly above-average individuals that performed software testing that most would find unglamorous. This team achieved more success than what anyone would ever expect. The success of the Black Team occurred because the formalized organization allowed the team to be themselves and did not force them to be restricted to the formalized procedures.

Why did IBM change some of their rules? IBM changed the rules for the Black Team in order to resolve the software defect problem. Customers, which are an external force, pushed IBM to resolve these software defects. This implies an open system. In order to understand what motivates organizations, we need to understand organizational paradigms. It is apparent that organizations will fall into several paradigms and will operate as a closed system at times, but will also fall into an open system as external forces affect its objectives. In IBM's case, cost savings and revenue generation were their objective and the customers' dissatisfaction was an external force affecting their decision-making. One would have to conclude that an understanding of organizational paradigms will enhance one's understanding of complex organizations.

Speech 4: Assessment of an IT Organization

Introduction: The evaluation and assessment of an IT organization within a company that we reviewed and analyzed during a consulting engagement reveled a maturity level overall that shows a beginning of the process (level 2) and moving towards the establishment of a process (level 3). The chart below will provide a summary of the maturity level scores for each of the six criteria. The evaluation reveals that this organization's current application portfolio and enterprise system has started the process to become more effective but still have a lot of room to grow. The strongest categories that show an establishment of a process toward a more effective IT organization include communications, governance, and technology scope. The weakest categories include competency/value measurements and skill areas that fall between "no alignment" and "beginning process." Each specific category is evaluated, analyzed, and synthesized throughout this discussion.

Communications Maturity: As Luftman (2003) points out, it is important for an organization's IT staff and management to have a clear understanding of the business organization which occurs with effective exchange of ideas and information. At this

organization, the IT department has made a good attempt to have continual user involvement in the strategic planning activities and encourages continual communication via user interviews, emails, and  phone conversations between the IT staff and user community during the analysis and design phases. A user contact is selected to work with an IT representative for each development project. This representative is usually a systems analyst. This process presents an understanding of business by some IT staff, usually limited to the systems analyst, and an understanding of IT by some non-IT staff, usually limited to those selected to work on the development project. This reveals an improved process toward alignment. In an effort to develop a formal business and IT strategic plan, the company had created an IT/business steering committee that is comprised of IT directors and the directors of the business units. This will present a strategic understanding among the IT management and business managers as a strategic IT plan is created for the year. However, the understanding is not always communicated to the IT staff as this resembles an effort to establish process according to Luftman. There are email and reports, along with formalized departmental training provided at This organization, especially in the area of Reservations and Group Development groups. There is a two way formalized communication style and ease of access in the area of the marketing and revenue functions within The company and seem to have some since of alignment with IT initiatives, training, and communication.

Other departmental groups are somewhat less aligned.
Considering that a lot of organizations have very little business
awareness on the part of IT or little appreciation of IT among
the business units according to Luftman, the company has
progressed further than these organizations and has moved into
the level of establishing a process. There are some factors that
show the company at a higher level in the area of
communication but there were some areas where they were
lower. The process of transmitting information between the
business unit and the IT staff is critical to develop a clear
alignment among the IT and business strategic initiatives. There
needs to be clear process of sending a message in such a way
that the message is received among both user and IT staff in as
close in meaning as possible to ensure the message is
understood. While the company has made a good effort in this
direction, they still have a lot of room to grow in this maturity
evaluation, but have at least achieved to a level 3 (establishing a
process).

Criterion	Score (Sub-Task)	Score (Major Category)
Communications		3.1
Understanding of business by IT	3.5	
Understanding of IT by business	3.0	
Organizational learning	4.0	
Style and ease of access		
Leveraging intellectual assets	2.0	
IT-business liaison	3.0	

Competency Maturity: Innovation is the utilization of new facts in an effort to adapt the directorial processes in order to construct feasible products and services. This is usually done by utilizing the latest technology, experimentation, creative insights, or even competitive information. It is necessary for the company to consider what degree of innovativeness to utilize as incremental innovation would be adopted to enhance existing practices and the implementation evolutionary applications. There are service levels established at the organization being evaluated for various IT commitments and the metrics are measured and evaluated. These service levels are not necessarily expressed in terms that are understandable to the business units at This organization. While the service levels are created based on specific criteria, clear rewards for surpassing the target levels or penalties for missing the target have not been established. According to Luftman, it is important to continuously assess the performance metrics criteria and determine how to continuously improve the overall environment. The company has began the process, but has not moved much further than establishing the initial levels and are basically limited to units within technology and not enterprise wide. IT metrics are reviewed for technical costs and the metrics are sometimes reviewed by the IT management but the investments in technology are rarely measured in the business sector unless large IT investments are made (excess of $1,000,000). There does not seem to be a linkage between the IT and business metrics. In this consideration, the maturity level of the company in the area of competency is at level 1 (with process, no alignment).

Criterion	Score (Sub-Task)	Score (Major Category)
Competency/Value Measurements		1.8
IT metrics	2.0	
Business metrics	1.0	
Link between IT and business metrics	1.0	
Service level agreements	2.0	
Benchmarking	2.5	
Formally assess IT investments	2.0	
Continuous improvement practices	2.0	

Governance Maturity: There is an IT strategy planning that is formalized with some business input and cross-functional planning through the utilization of an IT steering committee. The business strategic planning is formalized but is done at a unit functional level with only a slight input from the IT group. Both the IT and business metrics have intrinsic value to the organization but they do not link these metrics. The company has established a process considering that the CIO reports directly to the president of the company, which is the COO. According to McCall (2006), the current business environment is more complex than it was in the past and will continue to grow in its complexity. The complexity leads to new challenges by management from both internal and external environmental factors (p. 4). The author continues by indicating that each challenge must be broken into the seven key elements: (a)

People – development of knowledge and expertise to handle problems, (b) Business – understanding the niche market being serviced, (c) Society – responding to the changing needs of the customers, (d) Science – awareness and ability to exploit new opportunities, (e) Markets – ability to respond to the dynamics of the market place, (f) Technical – naturally tapping into the technical expertise, and (g) Wisdom – ability to understand historical thinking and applying holistic approaches within the organization. McCall (2006) continues to state that each organizational challenge will require its own spectrum within the application of these seven areas. Managers have to cope with the growing requirements dealing with regulation, intense competition, and brisk changes in the markets that threaten to overpower management. It is critical to face these challenges and respond to the changing dynamics with holistic management approaches (p. 5).

If organizations managed daily operations and make strategic decisions based only on historical data, a loss of opportunity would result as predictive and real-time indicators are a more effective way to manage strategy. According to Boudreaux (2006, January/February), technology is readily available to provide relevant information that is current and accurate. Enhancing business reporting can provide a structure for reporting information that is a model that incorporates all types of data, including significant indicators, instead of a historical snapshot. Business measurement of performance can provide all stakeholders with processed data that is necessary for better decisions (p. 24).   The organization being evaluated utilizes an executive dashboard process to create strategies of both business and IT, however, the business planning has limited input from IT and the IT planning has some business input along with cross functional planning.

Criterion	Score (Sub-Task)	Score (Major Category)
Governance		3.0
Formal business strategy planning	2.0	
Formal IT strategy planning	3.0	
Organizational structure	3.0	
Reporting relationships	3.0	
IT budgeting	3.0	
Rationale for IT spending	4.0	
Senior-level IT steering committee	3.0	
Prioritizing of IT projects	3.0	

Partnership Maturity: There is a perception among the business units that IT has become an asset to the organization by which a definite competitive advantage has been developed and has started to move towards establishing a process with some feeling that IT enables future business. The business community at the company does feel that the IT's role in strategic business planning is a process that does drive future processes, such as internet booking of reservations and availability to buy shore excursion packages on the internet. However, the IT department still appears to taking most risks with little rewards and does not appear to be changing in any time soon. The significant projects at the company have a selected business and IT sponsor assigned where a traditional transactional relationship exist.

Criterion	Score (Sub-Task)	Score (Major Category)
Partnership		2.6
Business perception of IT	2.5	
IT role in strategic business planning	3.0	
Shared risks and rewards	2.0	
Managing the IT-business relationship	3.0	
Relationship and trust style	2.0	
Business sponsors	3.0	

Technology Scope Maturity: The primary systems at the company enable future business activity as the significant lesson learned by the organization the realization of the importance for the core business system and the reservations application system is the core system to the company. This is the case as a travel industry organization will depend on the reservations as the most significant source of income. The standards were designed to enable business processes and are not always enforced. This organization started with the business process domain by evaluating the significant success that the reservations system has delivered to the business environment. This initial review of the process domain was necessary in order to reveal the responsiveness of the enterprise architecture that the company currently has built in an effort to meet the business objectives and needs of the organization. The organization continues to expand the enterprise network by constructing around the core reservations system by taking into account the information and knowledge domain, along with the organizational domain. After these domains were reviewed, the infrastructure domain was built and constructed to fully support the business strategic objectives and maintain the organization as a number one cruise operator in the world in an efficient and effective manner. In other words, the company maintained a successful legacy application as their core and built newer technology that interfaces well with the core application in order to meet the changing business environment. While there is an extensive enterprise system and infrastructure that has been built, the processes are not always followed and adhered even though the processes exist.

Criterion	Score (Sub-Task)	Score (Major Category)
Technology Scope		2.8
Primary systems	3.0	
Standards	2.0	
Architectural integration	3.0	
Perception of IT infrastructure	3.0	

Skills Maturity: The innovativeness and entrepreneurial environment at This organization's IT organization is somewhat encouraged at each unit level but not strongly encouraged and is not encouraged at a corporate level at all. Significant IT and human resource decisions are made by senior business and IT management for the organization. Change programs are somewhat emerging but there is still a significant amount of resistance and cross over opportunities rarely exist, as well as highly discouraged. The social interaction between IT and business units is mostly a business only type of relationship.

The IT hiring process is strictly focused on technical skills, as growth and retention process are almost non-existent. The maturity level of the organization in the area of skills is not quite a level 2.

Criterion	Score (Sub-Task)	Score (Major Category)
Skills		1.6
Innovative / Entrepreneurial environment	2.0	
Key IT/ HR Decisions	1.0	
Change readiness	1.5	
Career crossover opportunities	1.0	
Cross-functional opportunities	1.5	
Social interaction	2.0	
Attract and retain top talent	2.0	

Conclusion: The organization being evaluated have made some progress to achieve and sustain IT/business alignment, but have much more room to grow as they have begun the process and are moving towards the establishment of a process. The technology and business environments at the company are vast and dynamic as they are in the competitive travel industry market. The strongest categories that show an establishment of a process toward a more effective IT organization include communications, governance, and technology scope. The weakest categories include competency/value measurements and skill areas that fall between the "no alignment" and "beginning process" stages of maturity levels. The company should consider working on improving these two weak components in the near future which could have the potential of moving the alignment of the IT/business maturity toward establishing a process (Level 3).

Thoughts in Education

These are speeches relating to Dr. Michael Bird's thoughts on education and do not necessarily represent any institution philosophy that Dr. Bird may be affiliated with or their concurrence of such thoughts.

Speech 1: Personal Teaching Model

Introduction

I will review with you the various teaching philosophies and methodologies. After the discussion of such theories in the education of the adult learner, a model will be built and the adult instructor should consider the following: (a) encouraging self-direction, (b) integrating new information with previous experiences, (c) ensuring that the information will be seen as relevant and usable by the adult student, (d) practicing edutaining within the teaching process, and (e) ensuring proper assessment of students' performance with timely feedback. This is a model that will benefit the adult learner and ensure overall teaching effectiveness. Please consider that my talk does not necessary represent the university that I currently work at now or in the past. This is solely my perspectives and the institutions that I am or have been affiliated with may or may not agree with these perspectives.

Critical Reflective Teaching Principal

One must consider that a teacher needs to consider critical reflection within their educational presentations. Cunningham (1999) discusses the importance of becoming a reflective practitioner in order to overcome the turbulent challenges of marketing. Cunningham indicates that marketing teachers must become aware of the pedagogy trap and consider implement andragogy as they become a more critically reflective teacher. According to Ostorga (2006), teaching involves an interactive approach that requires a transformation through the years of experiences that actually promotes open-mindedness that will ultimately lead to the possibility of engaging on critical thought. An article by Feiman-Nemser (2001), states that a teacher following critical reflection will implement a process that infuses inquiry and action research in instructor preparation of courses, along with educative mentoring in field experiences (p. 17). This will set the actual stage for the initial phase of critical reflection development and good methods to promote proper critical thinking in reflective teachers. Therefore, we need to create a culture of reflection by identifying the value and contribution that all of us can bring, including both students and teacher. This leads us to participate in critical reflection for help in avoiding the traps of demoralization and self-laceration, as described by Brookfield. I would like to think we should perform an assumption analysis in such a manner that we will challenge our beliefs, values, cultural practices, and various social structures as we assess the actual impact these items have in our daily teaching processes. The next step is to realize that our assumptions are socially and personally created in a specific context based on our own historical events and cultural upbringing. The next step is imagining alternative methodologies of thinking in an effort to provide an opportunity to challenge our prevailing methodologies, and the final step is to become a skeptic reflectively. This will involve the questioning of universal truth claims or unexamined patterns of interaction through the prior three activities. In summary, Brookfield states that critical reflection is the ability to think about a subject so that the available evidence from that subject's field is suspended or temporarily rejected in order to establish the truth or viability of a proposition or action. It is important to determine that critical reflection involves the giving of reasons for decisions and events that take into account the broader historical, social, and political contexts.

According to Eisnebach, Golich, and Curry (1998), there are three notions mentioned of learning that appears to be a part of my thought process that include regular and repeated contact between instructor and student, recurrent feedback on student performance, and active learning. These authors further state that these three aspects help generate the student to assume responsibility for their learning as they enhance the overall quality of the learning process. At the university where I teach, these ideas are not only important but basically required. The contact between instructor and student include actual classroom time, office hours, twenty-four hour email contact, and regular postings within the threaded discussions (first notion or principle mentioned). The professors at some colleges and universities have to respond to emails within twenty-four hours, I generally do this faster whenever possible. The professor at these institutions generally must grade all assignments within seven days of the due date. These grades must include comments, especially if the student did not get full credit. This is included in the electronic gradebook within the online shell (e-College platform). I usually completed this within twenty-four to forty-eight hours. This timely feedback is important for students to learn and is evident by seeing how freshmen write and how it changes after their senior year (second notion or principle mentioned). I always utilize the experience in the work force as practical examples and relate them to the actual teaching objectives. My teaching methods include the use of both visual and non-visual techniques, while engaging the students in the classroom discussions an allow them to partake in an active part of the learning process.

Vella, Berardinelli, and Burrow (1998) points out that it is the responsibility of the instructors of adult learners to determine the best performance measures that well represents the learning process. I have done this by including several grading components including exams (30 to 40 percent), homework and assignments (30 to 35 percent), participation on threaded discussions (15 percent), participation in the classroom (5 to 10 percent), and oral presentations (5 to 15 percent). This should be a fair method to evaluate the adult learning process. These authors point out the five attributes of effective evaluation, which includes objectivity, identification of important learning elements, matching of evaluation to organizational philosophy, explicit and well-communicated measurement, and a focus on process as well as outcomes. I practice this, as well as, the utilization of a grading rubric for each assignment for objectivity, adaptability of each lesson to fit the learning capabilities of the current students, listing of grading criteria within the online syllabus, and the maintenance of objectivity by not looking at the name of a student while grading papers. Cross (1998) indicated that in a democratic and participatory environment, teachers and students can work together to negotiate objectives and assessment methods. However, at most traditional and non-progressive colleges and universities, this is not permitted or practiced. Generally, the instructors must have the syllabus completed forty-eight hours before the first day of class. Therefore, the students do not participate on this type of negotiation. The instructor can overcome this restriction by adjusting some of the course assignments outlined on the syllabus to better fit the students' needs and objectives. Also, the syllabus can be adjusted in future semesters.

This previous discussion presents the lenses required to improve critical reflection in teaching effectiveness, which is autobiography (relating our own experiences), our student's eyes (incorporating our students' experiences), colleague's experiences (incorporating experiences of our peers), and literature review (incorporating various theories of teaching). All of these lenses are necessary in order to build a model applicable for modern style of teaching adult learners.

Review of Theories and the Rise of Andragogy

There have been many theories of education starting with the classical theories of classical conditioning, behaviorism, and connectionism. Pavlov used classical conditioning by involving stimulus and response learning which was reinforced through extinction, generalization, and differentiation. A bridge started to be built between the classical views of learning to the contemporary. Skinner extended the behaviorism theory through reinforcement by involving the utilization of operant conditioning, along with a promotion of the use of positive reinforcement and negative punishment. These theories of extending behaviorism were also expanded by Hull and Guthrie where learner involvement contributed to a visual style of learning (Guthrie) and influencing of a response that arise after a stimulus via connectionism (Hull). Dewey, Tolman, and Maslow build the bridge towards contemporary styles of teaching by presenting more independence and self control through learner and teacher interaction, providing a path towards the objective, and then presentation of learning based on motivation and personality. This bridge went through a learner involvement phase through a learner oriented phase of teaching theories. Piaget and Bruner presented the first thoughts of contemporary learning theories where total learner involvement was thought to lead to reflection. This model was the utilization of cognition with evolutionary stages which provides an evolutionary development with the stages moving progressively complex with an emphasis on cognitive skills of the learners. These will ultimately to lead to a model developed by Knowles that presented the need to gain knowledge as the learner's self concept is developed through the readiness to learn with one's role of experience, which is called the andragogical model. According to Knowles (1984), andragogy is the philosophy that attempts to clarify why adults learn differently than other types of students. According to Cross (1981), adults have a tendency to hunt for knowledge opportunities because life changes serve as their incentive and inspiration. These life changes include divorce, marriage, job termination or changes, retirement, or moving to different geographic locations. In order to deal with these life changes, adults tend to want a learning experience that will provide them with an opportunity to better their job position or make a transformation for an enhancement within their life. In other words adults are not only interested in knowledge for the sake of knowledge but they see learning as a means to an end and not an end in itself. According to Zemke (1984), there is a wealth of information and experiences that is brought to the learning environment by these adult learners and they would like to be thought of as an equal as they direct themselves into the educational process.

First, as one looks at the demands of learning, the adult learner must balance life responsibilities with the demands of learning (andragogy) and younger students devote more time to the demands of learning because their main responsibilities are minimal (pedagogy). Adult learners are more autonomous and self directed leaving the role of instructors as mostly a guide for them in their own knowledge process rather than supplying them with the raw facts. In pedagogy, the role of instructor is direct and the learning process is fact based lecturing. Budd and Freeman further presents that there are actually four principals in andragogy that reflect this difference between andragogy and pedagogy, which are: (a) changes in self-concept: maturity brings a shift from dependency to self-direction; (b) the role of experience: maturity brings a reservoir of experiences that can be a resource for learning; (c) readiness to learn: learning readiness in an adult is oriented more toward one's social role; and (d) orientation to learning: maturity brings an orientation towards learning that is more problem-centered.

Reasons for Why Adults Learn Differently

Lucas also presented that the process of learning becomes at least as important as the content. Adults need to be clear as to the reason why they need to learn something and tend to prefer solving problems and want to participate in experience learning. The instructor's role becomes that of a facilitator instead of a lecturer with the following factors: (a) adults can be easily intimidated by formal learning experiences especially if they have unfavorable educational memories as children, (b) adults tend to have more experiences in life that they want to share, (c) adults tend to see learning as a social type of activity, (d) adults tend to have differing priorities based upon their age and stage within their life cycle, and (e) adults tend to need more feedback.

An example of andragogy can be found in police training. Birzer (2003) indicates that when the theory of andragogy is incorporated into police training, there is evidence of closing the gaps noted in the learning process in the police training classroom that has haunted police training authorities. Traditionally, the preponderance of subject matter in the police-training atmosphere has been taught utilizing behavioral approaches which may not be effective when teaching an evolving police curriculum which has been implemented under the axiom of community-policing. As Andragogy has started to increase in its overall popularity as an educational and effective training method, many organizational institutions have implemented many of these components with greater success for adult education and training. This has been evident in Birzer's research of police training initiatives.

Principals of Teaching Adult Learners

As andragogy focuses on real-life application and problem solving capacity that has proven training effectiveness among adult learners, we will summarize the best methods to teach adult learners, based on Aik and Tway (2006), Margerison (2005, December), Song, Sviatoslav, and Braynov (2004), and Notten (2002). The instructor of adult learners should consider utilizing problem oriented instruction such as simulations, case studies, and problem solving teams as these make learning more relevant to real-life experiences. The actual instruction should be more about tasks instead of memorization of content, while the instructor will need to place their own egos aside, give up some control, and not fear to have their ideas challenged by the adult learner. It is important to make the learning environment comfortable while allowing for reasonable breaks for the adult learner to collect their thoughts and handle the real-life situations they are balancing. When providing examinations, the instructors should consider the use of open ended questions to bring out the vast experiences of the adult learners. The four principals of adult learning, based on this research, include (a) letting the adult learners direct themselves within the educational experience, (b) integrating new information with previous experiences, (c) ensuring that the information will be seen as relevant to the adult learner, and (d) assuring that the information is easily usable by the adult learner in their real-life situations. Having students direct the learning process with their own experiences can aid in the accomplishment of this objective. This is where andragogy can become the art and science of adult education, where the learning process concentrates on these real-life applications as it emphasizes that the adult training effectiveness is enhanced though the learners' actual performance of the task. For example, the seniors must manage an actual project at the university that I have taught at through one of their business partners within a fifteen week period prior to graduating. This type of learning process actually ends up focusing on the students' real-life application and problem-solving capacity. Overall, the workplace of these business partners of the university can provide an excellent atmosphere for facilitating individual learning through authentic, goal-directed activities, and everyday engagement in problem solving.

Humor in Education

The working adult student has to wake up early in the morning, commute to the job, work eight to nine hours, and then attend a three to four hour lecture at night. Most of these students have families and bills to be concerned about. While including real-world experiences is important, the instructor must be able to keep students interest by including an entertaining and teaching combination. Therefore, the instructor entertains the students while providing an education and meeting the course objectives. An important teaching technique of education is to use variety, by utilizing various mediums such as video, in-class skits, demonstrations, and Power Point slides along with lectures. Within the lecture, the instructor can add comedy and discussions of personal experiences of the professor or students. I believe that this would make Knowles theory even more complete.

The research on humor in teaching conducted by Torok, McMorris, and Lin (2004) was a great research study. The authors conducted a study to determine the students' perceptions regarding the use of various types of humor by the professors within the classroom setting. The types of humor were also evaluated by the researchers, as well. This research examined the methods utilized with the perceived effectiveness and competence, along with the perceptions of whether or not the students learning experience was improved, reduced, or stayed the same. The authors were able to conclude that when humor was utilized within the classroom setting, it had the potential to humanize, illustrate, defuse, encourage, reduce anxiety, and keep the students thinking. It also aided in helping students to stay focused in long lecture classroom settings. At this point adding humor in distance learning is difficult and requires further research.

I would also add that the Berk (2000) study on how humor in course tests can reduce anxiety and improve overall performance was another article that fits my style. The overall purpose of this article is to present updated information on the research that the author conducted regarding humor in courses. The study reveals a reduction in student anxiety and an improvement in the overall student performance, as it presents some ideal techniques to utilizing humor in courses. The research question on hand was "does adding humor in course tests reduce anxiety among students taking the test and as a result improve student performance? The author conducted a six year case analysis study, along with some interviews, among both graduate and undergraduate students. The study seems to suggest and the author concludes that the students under this six year study have found that students which tend to feel humor on course tests aid in the reduction of anxiety, decrease overall stress in the test taking process, and improves the student's overall performance. The author further concludes that the psychological and physiological research findings that he conducted and the processed data collected was sufficient to provide evidence that humor definitely decreases overall anxiety, tension, and stress that normally exist while students are taking course tests. He also concludes that student's performance is improved. I like the fact that this was a six year study for this mixed research strategy and if its results should be adequate enough to present some sense of relevance to this research question.

Application of Theories in Building a Model

According to the research study performed by Lord, Shelly, and Zimmerman (2007), over ninety percent of students tend to better understand the nature of science experiments after creating their own lab investigations and seventy-five percent understand the procedures involved in the discovery when they had to design their own experiment. This appears to support my model of encouraging self direction and allowing the adult student to diagnose their needs, formulate specific learning objectives, choose appropriate learning strategies, and select the resources needed for learning as they tailor the projects to fit their specific needs. Knowles philosophy of andragogy also develops for the first principal of a model and has been validated by many other authors besides Lord, Shelly, and Zimmerman.

Margerison, (2005, December), along with Kemp and O'Keefe (2003), appear to support the ideology of integrating previous experiences from the instructor, as well as from the students, in order to create a value added learning environment and ensuring students can see a clear picture of the overall course objectives. These authors, along with Knowles, appear to help build the second and third principals of the model where the instructor should integrate new information with previous experiences of both the instructor and students, especially where relevancy to the lecture appears appropriate. With the Berk study, along with the Torok, McMorris, and Wen-Chi study, regarding humor, there seems to be support to the Bird article regarding combining education and entertaining in the adult learning environment (fourth principal). This would also be an important part to a more modernized teaching model.

Several authors have supported the idea that the instructor should consider the process of assessment (fifth principal) as an ongoing process targeted at the comprehension and improvement of the student learning process. Palmer (1998) discusses the importance of assessment in adult education. According to Catt, Stephen, Miller, Donald, and Schallenkamp (2007), as well as many other authors reviewed in the development of this model development, has stated that the student assessment and feedback process is a required component of teaching effectiveness. It is important for the assessment to be manageable and utilized a process to measure student performance, as well as to measure the overall effectiveness of instructional delivery. Based on these theories and thoughts of critical reflection a model can be developed.

Conclusion

According to Kemp and O'Keefe (2003), the importance of a university or college is not only plan for curriculum, program, and facility improvement, but also to consider the continual improvement of the faculty. These authors discuss continuous improvement processes such as mentorship programs and a program for the enhancement of teaching, which is an aim to focus the attention of the faculty on the university's commitment to the excellence of teaching. Therefore, this model should be considered an initial blueprint for an adult instructor. Then, the instructor and instructional institutions could consider refreshing this model and improve upon it on periodic basis, based on student feedback and observations of the overall success of the learning performance. Therefore, the instructor should consider the following model: (a) encouraging self-direction, (b) integrating new information with previous experiences, (c) ensuring that the information will be seen as relevant and usable by the adult student, (d) practicing edutaining within the teaching process, and (e) ensuring proper assessment of the students' performance with timely feedback. This is a model that will benefit the adult learner and ensure overall teaching effectiveness, while incorporating the four lenses of reflection, which includes autobiography, our student's eyes, colleague's experiences, and literature review.

Speech 2: *Surviving an Awful Professor*

When I was a student at the University of South Florida back in 1980, I took an English class called, "Advanced Expository Writing." The completion of six essay papers with 1000 to 1500 words each was the requirement to complete this course. Prior to this course, I had received two A's in my previous collegiate English classes, but this new class proved to be a true challenge for me.

My first essay was an argumentative paper and I began by attempting to be an expert on the topic that I had chosen. I utilized the school library as I researched both books and journals that were on microfilm. Yes, the days of electronic databases and the Internet were not in existence back then. However, I was still able to immerse myself in the words of the great thinkers of the chosen topic by taking good notes from the research materials. With this knowledge, I analyzed the facts, opinions, and justifications regarding my research and then organized the data on index cards. I wrote down the evidence, reasons, and definitions of the claims by the authors. I looked for the strengths and weaknesses as I analyzed how I should write this paper.

I then came up with a thesis statement for my main point that was easy to write the entire essay around. I created an outline from the index cards and then wrote out my rough draft. After editing my work, I then typed the essay on my electric typespeaker. Believe it or not, there were not any personal computers back in those days and I was considered technologically advanced with my electric typespeaker.

I started the paper with an introduction that was designed to set the stage of bringing the reader into my essay's argument. I continued writing by carefully developing my paragraphs and then provided a flowing conclusion. This whole process took me around twelve hours over three days. I was proud of my accomplishment and was so sure that it was an "A" paper.

When I received my graded paper back, I was surprised to see a big fat "C-"on the paper without any explanation. My professor was notorious for being a tough grader and did not believe in providing any comments because she wanted the student to make an appointment to see her. Upon my visit, she pointed to one word on the paper and said that was the only reason I received that grade. The word was "conflagration" which means "fire." Then, she asked me what was the purpose of writing a paper and I said it was to communicate your thoughts and ideas. She said that was correct but I excluded about 95 percent of the readers by using a word such as "conflagration" instead of just coming out and saying "fire". I walked out mad and complained to other students about how this professor was an awful instructor.

Of course, I started to write my papers without using the big words and this experience also helped me as I moved to the field of Information Technology. By thinking back to this professor, I kept my explanations and presentations simple enough for the business users and management to understand. These individuals were not technology experts and needed to understand the process at a much simpler level. This ability to speak with the technology experts and business users was a great asset in my career path.

In conclusion, the awful English professor had actually taught me more than how to write but also how to speak at a level for others to understand. This also has helped me in my current career as a professor as I now have the ability to break the components down to help students understand the concepts being taught. Thank goodness that I had this awful English professor who gave me a low grade on what I thought was an "A" paper.

Speech 3: *Being Judged Incorrectly*

Many people have faced obstacles in their lives as a child and as an adult. Let me share a story with you about my first school experience. When I was six years old, I was enrolled by my parents to attend first grade in the public school system in South Miami Heights. This would be my first true opportunity to interact with children my own age. I did start pre-school in the past but had to withdraw after two weeks due to a severe hip injury but that is another story.

I was interviewed by the first grade teachers to determine my placement. The teachers immediately recommended me for a special education class because they felt that I was behind what a first grader would know and further testing was not required. My mother did not stand for this judgment because she knew that being placed in these special education classes would label me unfairly for my educational career. The teachers determined this because the way I talked. I was born with defect in the way my tongue was formed which could have been a result of being born three weeks early. I could not say anything with an "R", "SH", or "CH" in a way that one could understand me because I could not form my tongue correctly. This is what one would call a speech impediment but does not mean that I was behind what a first grader should know. My mother knew this and wanted me to be tested further. The teachers protested because they said that I would just get frustrated and will harm me in the end. However, the principal gave in due to my mother's persistence.

I took the math and reading test in the principal's office. I finished the math test and scored on a level of a third grader. I finished the reading test and scored on a level of a second grader. It was obvious that my mother had worked with me for several years and just because I could not talk well due to a speech impediment, I should be placed in a special education class. As a matter of fact, the principal recommended me to be placed in the advanced class. The teacher for the advanced class was furious.

After attending the advanced first grade class for two weeks, the teacher insisted that a school psychologist test my IQ. After this test, I scored an IQ of 129 which is above the average that falls between 85 and 115. While I was not considered highly gifted, I was considered above average and my placement in the advanced first grade class was considered proper. Therefore, the teacher had to keep me in her class. However, the school psychologist did recommend a professional speech therapist.

After four years of speech therapy, I was able to learn how to improve my speaking and was able to pronounce words with an "R", "SH", or "CH" in it. In four years, the therapist showed me how I can compensate for my tongue defect. By the time I finished first grade, I was reading on a third grade level and performing math skills on a fifth grade level. Therefore, do not let others tell you that you cannot succeed. Keep the faith in pursuing your dreams of education and career paths. It is up to you to overlook the obstacles and be persistent in you overall goals. I succeeded in first grade even though I was judged incorrectly and obstacles were placed in front of me. Of course, I have to give many thanks to my mom for having faith in me.

Speech 4: *Incorporating Entertainment into Education*

Humor in education is a method of entertaining students while providing a quality education. As a college professor, it can be difficult to obtain and maintain our students' attention, especially for classes lasting up to four hours at a time. Sometimes, it seems as if learning goes down the drain as students appear drowsy, non-responsive, and non-engaged. Some students appear to take up space and do not seem enthused to learn after all your hard efforts as a professional educator.

In the seventies and eighties, it was not unusual for college students to attend and listen to a two- to four-hour class being taught. In today's educational arena, students can't maintain their attention throughout an entire two- to four hour-class lecture. – How have students changed?

First, we should discuss the types of students that exist in today's world. There are the full-time students who are young (18 to 25) and attend classes during the day. There are also those students who are older, work all day, and attend night classes.

Next, we need to understand why students are easily distracted. The younger, full-time students grew up in an age of instant gratification. Most of their childhood life included cable or satellite television with access to over sixty channels, video games, internet availability, and a lot of entertainment opportunities. If one mode of entertainment starts to bore them; they easily change to another mode of entertainment.

How would these students tolerate a four-hour lecture without any variety? What would be their motivating factor?

The working adult student has to wake up early in the morning, commute to the job, work eight to nine hours, and then attend a three to four hour lecture at night. Most of these students have families and bills to be concerned about. How can these students handle a straight four-hour lecture?

Both of these types of students can easily become bored and end up tuning out a large portion of a lecture. As instructors, we must obtain and maintain their attention in order to achieve our goal of teaching. How can this be accomplished?

An instructor should become an "Edutainer," where the instructor entertains the students while providing an education and meeting the course objectives. An important teaching technique of education is to use variety, by utilizing various mediums such as video, in-class skits, demonstrations, and Power Point slides along with lectures. Within the lecture, the instructor can add comedy and discussions of personal experiences of the professor or students.

Here is an outline of how a professor can improve the overall learning experience and become an edutainer.

Edutaining Step 1: Show videos that add value while entertaining. Incorporating medium such as videos or DVDs will enhance the learning experience, provided that they are not boring. There are some videos that provide valuable learning experience while entertaining. For example, The Billion Dollar Bubble released in 1976 provides an entertaining account of the Equity Funding fraud case with its chairman, Stanley Goldblum, in the early 1970s. The video reflects a large corporate fraud as it presents the true story of the $2 billion insurance fraud scandal of the Equity Funding Corporation of America. The methods utilized in this bogus insurance scheme, the reasons behind the fraud, and the callous attitude among the management are highlighted in this video. The film runtime is sixty minutes and stars Sam Wanamaker and James Woods. The runtime is perfect for a four-hour class and will generate much class discussion.

There are several videos or DVDs that are available with similar attributes. Adding this type of medium should not replace the lecture environment, but help enhance the overall learning experience. The key is to consider the film length, how it is presented, and timing.

Edutaining Step 2: Involve students in skits. The instructor can set up a scenario that corresponds with the lecture and select students to participate. Once the students understand the scenario, the instructor lets the students execute the scenario. Then, the class is encouraged to analyze the skit as portrayed by the participating students. The discussion should be tied to the lesson provided by the lecture.

Edutaining Step 3: Conduct an impromptu satire. The instructor should consider performing an impromptu satire to provide an element of surprise. An example would include the performance of an impromptu satire prior to a chapter discussing Operations Management in an Introduction to Business class. In this illustration, the instructor takes a garbage can and walks throughout the classroom collecting items to place in the garbage can. By repeating the steps in collecting the items, the instructor clearly demonstrates inefficiency. This then leads to analysis and discussion of what inefficiency is and how it can be avoided. Once this discussion has been completed, the instructor can easily flow into the chapter subject matter to be covered in class. -The element of surprise from these types of satire enhances the learning experience.

Edutaining Step 4: Add demonstrations with scenarios. The instructor should consider adding demonstrations of related subject matter that include job-related scenarios, case study analysis, or any other type of demonstration. For example, a Marketing class could include a demonstration of a soda taste test and a Management class could include a case study analysis of a real-life business situation that could lead to class discussion.

Edutaining Step 5: Add some jazz to the Power Point slides. If the instructor isn't careful, Power Point slides can become boring. It is important to add some flavor to otherwise boring slides by adding pictures, sound effects, movie clips, and surprise slides. Including pictures with cartoon figures and animals that relate to the subject matter make it more interesting; students will be more inclined to pay attention to the lecture. As the instructor defines money and money supply, for example, the instructor should consider a funny picture of an animal with a wallet in order to keep the interest of the students. Adding short movie clips and sound effects that relate to the subject matter will also keep students interested in the slide presentation. Having surprise slides such as unexpected music, picture, and/or sound will keep students awake and interested in the presentation of the subject material. A database instructor may feel that database design is interesting, but the students may not have the same passion.

Edutaining Step 6: Make the lecture more interesting by adding flair. This can be accomplished by including voice changes, comedy, and facial expressions. Changing voice pitch occasionally during the lecture will help emphasize key points and prevent a "monotone syndrome." When students constantly hear the same pitch in a professor's voice, it becomes hypnotic and makes it hard for the students to stay focused. Changes in pitch keep the students interested. Impromptu and planned comedy within the lecture will also hold the students' interest. It is important to keep comedy short and related to the subject matter or relevant to the situation. Short comedy routines or even one-liners are best. To add even more interest, adding simple facial expressions can help.

Edutaining Step 7: Make the lecture more interesting by adding work-related examples. Using previous work or life experiences that are relevant to the lecture can add value and help the students understand the lesson being taught. The instructor can solicit experiences from the class that relate to the lesson. This will help ensure that the students feel engaged in the learning process.

Edutaining Step 8: Make the lecture more interesting by engaging all students. Inviting the students to talk and discuss the topics being taught will help ensure students' interest. The instructor should call on the students by name and have them present answers to questions asked. If a student gives an incorrect answer, it is important to not put a student down. The instructor should give encouragement and move onto a better answer. Engaging students and providing encouragement will help keep students interested and involved during the lecture.

While all these steps help enhance the lecture process, there are some simple rules to remember in order to not lose control in the classroom. It is critical not to overdo any particular technique and the instructor must remember that some of them may not be appropriate for all lessons. The instructor should strategically utilize these steps within the lesson plans and, most importantly, be natural in the delivery process. Also, the instructor should not try to change their teaching style overnight. It is best to start slowly.

I have utilized these methods in my teaching delivery style and have noticed much success. Students have indicated that they learn better in this type of environment and look for classes taught by either me or other professors following a similar style.

It is important to provide an education and have the students learn, but when we both educate and entertain, we are more successful at teaching the subject material and holding the students' interest longer. Regardless of whether the subject is database, management, or world history, it can become more interesting with edutaining. This speaker believes the addition of edutaining would make Knowles theory described in chapter one even more complete.

It is important to discuss further the importance of humor in education. The research on humor in teaching conducted by Torok, McMorris, and Lin (2004) was a great research study. The authors conducted a study to determine the students' perceptions regarding the use of various types of humor by the professors within the classroom setting. The types of humor were also evaluated by the researchers, as well. This research examined the methods utilized with the perceived effectiveness and competence, along with the perceptions of whether or not the students learning experience was improved, reduced, or stayed the same. The authors were able to conclude that when humor was utilized within the classroom setting, it had the potential to humanize, illustrate, defuse, encourage, reduce anxiety, and keep the students thinking. It also aided in helping students to stay focused in long lecture classroom settings. At this point adding humor in distance learning is difficult and requires further research.

This speaker would also add that the Berk (2000) study on how humor in course tests can reduce anxiety and improve overall performance was another article that fits my style. The overall purpose of this article is to present updated information on the research that the author conducted regarding humor in courses. The study reveals a reduction in student anxiety and an improvement in the overall student performance, as it presents some ideal techniques to utilizing humor in courses. The research question on hand was "does adding humor in course tests reduce anxiety among students taking the test and as a result improve student performance? The author conducted a six year case analysis study, along with some interviews, among both graduate and undergraduate students. The study seems to suggest and the author concludes that the students under this six year study have found that students which tend to feel humor on course tests aid in the reduction of anxiety, decrease overall stress in the test taking process, and improves the student's overall performance. The author further concludes that the psychological and physiological research findings that he conducted and the processed data collected was sufficient to provide evidence that humor definitely decreases overall anxiety, tension, and stress that normally exist while students are taking course tests. He also concludes that student's performance is improved. This speaker likes the fact that this was a six year study for this mixed research strategy and if its results should be adequate enough to present some sense of relevance to this research question.

References

Aik, Chong Tek & Tway, Duane C. (2006). Elements and
    principles of training as a performance improvement
    solution. *Performance Improvement*, *45*(3), 28-32.
    Retrieved August 31, 2007, from ABI/INFORM
    Global database. (Document ID: 1001341771).

Alcione N Ostorga (2006). Developing teachers who are
    reflective practitioners: A complex process. *Issues in
    Teacher Education*, *15*(2), 5-20. Retrieved August 31,
    2007, from ProQuest Education Journals database.
    (Document ID: 1302647501).

Andrea, Carugati & Elias, Hadzilias (2007, April-June).
    Development of E-government services for cultural
    heritage: Examining the key dimensions. International
    Journal of Technology and Human Interaction, 3, 2, 45-
    70.

Avdin, Mehmet, Harmsen, Frank, van Slooten, Kees, & Stegwee,
    Robert (2005, October-December). On the adaptation
    of an agile information systems development method.
    Journal of Database Management, 16, 4, 24-40.

Balmelli, L. Brown, D, & Cantor, M. (2006, July) Model-driven
    systems development. IBM Systems Journal, 45, 3, 569.

Barua, A., Kriebel, H.C.& Mukhopadhyay, T. (1995). Information
    technologies and business value: An analytic and
    empirical investigation. Information Systems Research,
    6, 1, 3-23.

Batchelor, Rick (2005, October). Executive dashboard: A
    decision maker's favorite. Franchise World, 37, 10, 27-
    31.

Becker, William (1998, May). Engaging students in quantitative
analysis with short case examples from the academic
and popular press. The American Economic Review, 88,
2, 480-486.

Bennett-Alexander, Dawn D (2009). Employment Law for
Business, 6th Ed. McGraw-Hill Learning Solutions.

Bennett-Alexander, Dawn D (2009). Employment Law for
Business, 6th Ed. McGraw-Hill Learning Solutions.

Bennett-Alexander, Dawn D.. Employment Law For Business. 6.
VitalSource Bookshelf. McGraw-Hill Learning Solutions,
2009, Tuesday, July 15, 2012.
http://online.vitalsource.com/books/0077588967

Berk, Ronald A. (2000). Does humor in course tests reduce
anxiety and improve performance? *College Teaching*,
48(4), 151-8. Retrieved August 11, 2007, from Wilson
Education Abstracts database. (Document ID:
64590364).

Bird, P. M. (2007, June 15). *Edutaining: Creating interest in the
classroom*.
Retrieved August 11, 2007, from
http://professormbird.com/page5.html.

Birzer, Michael (2003). The theory of andragogy applied to
police training. *Policing*, *26*(1), 29-42. Retrieved August
31, 2007, from Research Library database. (Document
ID: 334603151).

Bisson, Simon (2004, November 4). Life: Inside IT: Taken to
extremes: Simon Bisson explores the world of eXtreme
Programming, which emphasizes collaboration and
flexibility over rigid processes. The Guardian, 16.

Blackler, F.H. M. & Brown, C. A., (1983, July). Qualitative research and paradigms of practice. The Journal of Management Studies, 20, 3, 349-365.

Boehm, Barry (2006). A view of 20th and 21st century software engineering. International Conference on Software Engineering: Keynotes Talks, 12-29.

Boudreaux, Caroline (2006, January/February). Enhanced business reporting: Providing relevant information for decision makers. Catalyst, 24-29.

Boudreaux, Caroline (2006, January/February). Enhanced business reporting: Providing relevant information for decision makers. *Catalyst*, 24-29.

Brookfleild, S. (1995). *Becoming a Critically Reflective Teacher*. San Francisco: Jossey-Bass Higher and Adult Education Series.

Browne, Beverly A, Kaldenberg, Dennis, Brown, Daniel J. (1992-1993, Winter). Games people play: A comparative study of promotional game participants and gamblers. Journal of Applied Business Research, 9, 1; 93-99.

Budd, Clair & Freeman, Ronald (2004). JohnWesley meets Malcolm Knowles: was the class meeting andragogical? *Christian Education Journal, 1*(3), 63-79. Retrieved August 31, 2007, from ProQuest Education Journals database. (Document ID: 751535101).

Buss, Dale (2007, March). Winning with global value chains. Chief Executive, 28-32.

Buxbaum, Peter (2001, May 7). Measuring alignment. Computerworld, 35, 19, 46.

Byrd, T. A. & Marshall, T. E. (1997). Relating information technology investment to organizational performance: a causal model. Omega, 25, 1, 43-56.

Calvert, David (1996, June 5). Rapid application development. The University of Guelph.

Canfora, Gerardo, Cimitile, Aniello, Garcia, Felix, Piattini, Mario, & Visaggio, Corrado Aaron (2007, August). Evaluating performances of pair designing in industry. The Journal of Systems and Software, 80, 8, 1317.

Carayannis, Elias & Alexander. Jeffrey (1999, August). Winning by co-opeting in strategic government-university-industry R&D partnerships: The power of complex, dynamic knowledge networks. Journal of Technology Transfer, 24, 2-3; 197.

Carper, D. L., McKinsey, J. A., & West, B. W. (2007). Understanding the Law. Mason: Thomsan Learning.

Catt, Stephen, Miller, Donald, & Schallenkamp, Ken (2007). You are the key: communicate for learning effectiveness. *Education, 127*(3), 369-377. Retrieved August 18, 2007, from Wilson Education Abstracts database. (Document ID: 1268062591).

Cowham, Robert, & Stephens, Matt (2005, March). To XP or not to XP? IT Now, 47, 2, 16.

Cross, K. Patricia. 1981.*Adults as learners: Increasing participation and facilitating learning.* San Francisco: Jossey-Bass.

Cuffe, Stanford (2005). Future e-business models and strategies for managers. Futurics, 29, ½, 41-46.

Cunningham, A. C. (1999). Commentary Confessions of a reflective practitioner: meeting the challenges of marketing's destruction. *European Journal of Marketing*, *33*(7/8), 685-697. Retrieved August 31, 2007, from ABI/INFORM Global database. (Document ID: 115924936).

Davis, Gordon, Ein-Dor, Phillip, King, William, & Torkzadeh (2006). IT offshoring: History, prospects, and challenges. Journal of the Association for Information Systems, 7, 11, 770-795.

Dessureault, S., Porter, J., & Woodhall, M. (2004, January). Data integration for information technology infrastructure in mining. CIM Bulletin, 97, 1076, 49-56.

Devaraj, S. & Kohli, R. (2000). Information technology payoff in the healthcare industry: a longitudinal study. Journal of Management Information Systems, Vol. 16 No. 4, pp. 41-67.

Dewhurst, Frank, Martínez-Lorente, Angel Rafael, and Sánchez-Rodríguez, Cristobal (2003). An initial assessment of the influence of IT on TQM: A multiple case study. International Journal of Operations and Production Management, 23, 4, 348-374.

Donlon, J. P. (2007, March). Ensuring a healthy value chain. Chief Executive, 224, 34-39.

Downey, H. Kirk, Ireland, R. Duane. (1979, December). Quantitative versus qualitative: Environmental assessment in organizational studies. Administrative Science Quarterly, 24, 4, 630.

EEOC Website (n.d.). Questions and Answers on the Final Rule Implementing the ADA Amendments Act of 2008. Retrieved on August 12, 2012 from

http://www.eeoc.gov/laws/regulations/ada_qa_final_r
ule.cfm.

Eisenbach, R., Golich,V., & Curry, R (1998). Classroom
assessment across the disciplines. *New Directions for
Teaching and Learning.* 75, 59-66.

Eva, Malcolm (2001, December). Requirements acquisition for
rapid applications development. Information and
Management, 39, 2, 101.

Evans, Daniel, & Smith, Aaron (2004). Augmenting the value
chain: Identifying competitive advantage via the
internet. Journal of Information Technology Theory and
Application, 6, 1, 61-78.

Feiman-Nemser, S. (2001). Helping novice teachers to teach.
Journal of Teacher Education 52(1), 17.

Fondiler, David (2005, December 29). Marakon global study
finds big opportunity to improve strategic decision-
making at most companies [Electronic]. Business Wire,
1.

Francis, Diane (2005, October 25). The case for disruptive
innovation: Companies that cannot adapt ultimately
fail. National Post, FP 2.

Free Legal Advice Website (n.d.). Can an employee be on call
without pay. Retrieved on August 17, 2012 from
http://forum.freeadvice.com/wage-salary-issues-
96/can-employee-call-without-pay-538387.html.

Gable, Guy (1994, April). Integrating case study and survey
research methods: An example in information systems.
European Journal of Information Systems, 3, 2, 112-126.

Glen, P. (2003). *Leading geeks: How to manage and lead people who deliver technology*. San Francisco: Jossey-Bass.

Gniewosz, G. (1990, Summer). The share investment decision process and information use: An exploratory case study. Accounting and Business Research, 20, 79, 223-230.

Grace, Pauline (2002). Contemporary issues in human resource management: Gaining a competitive advantage. Human Resource Management Journal, 12, 1, 98-99.

Gregg, Bob (n.d.). Obesity is a disability, says EEOC, Diversity Incorporated Website. Retrieved on August 11, 2012 from http://www.diversityinc.com/diversity-and-inclusion/obesity-is-a-disability-says-eeoc/.

Gummesson, Evert (2006). Qualitative research in management: addressing complexity, context and persona. Management Decision, 44, 2, 167-179.

Hara, Katsuko (1995). Quantitative and qualitative research approaches in education. Education, 115, 351-355.

Harrigan, Anne & Vincenti, Virginia. (2004). Developing higher-order thinking through an intercultural assignment: A scholarship of teaching inquiry project. *College Teaching, 52*(3), 113-120. Retrieved August 11, 2007, from Wilson Education Abstracts database. (Document ID: 660919931).

Hilkka, Merisalo-Rantanen, Tuure, Tuunanen, & Matti, Rossi (2005, October-December). Journal of Database Management, 16, 4, 41-61.

Hill, Frances & Collins, Lee. (1999, January). The quality management of business process reengineering: A study of incremental and radical approaches to change management at BTNI. Total Quality Management, 10, 1, 37-45.

Holmstrom, Helena, Fitzgerald, Brian, Agerfalk, Par, & Conchuir, Eoin (2006, Summer). Agile practices reduce distance in global software development. Information Systems Management, 23, 3, 7-28.

Howard, Alan (1997). A new RAD-based approach to commercial information systems development: The dynamic system development method. Industrial Management, 97, 5, 175.

Hsiao, R.L. and Ormerod, R.J. (1998). A new perspective on the dynamics of information technology-enabled strategic change, Information Systems Journal, 8, 21-52.

Hurmerinta-Peltomaki, Leila & Nummela, Niina (2006). Mixed methods in international business research: A value-added perspective. Management International Review, 46, 4, 439-459.

Hyde, A. (1992). The proverbs of total quality management: Re-charting the path to quality improvement in the public sector. Public Productivity and Management Review, 16, 1, 25-37.

Jabnoun, Naceur & Sahraoui, Sofiane (2004). Enabling a TQM structure through Information Technology. Competitiveness Review, 14, 1/2; 72-81.

Johnson, R. L. (2006, Summer). Strategy, success, a dynamic economy and the 21st century manager. The Business Review, 5(2), 23-29.

Katz, D. & Kahn R. L. (1966). *The social psychology of organizations*. New York: Wiley.

Kavanagh, Donncha & Kelly, Seamas (2002, July). Sensemaking, safety, and situated communities in contemporary networks. Journal of Business Research, 55, 7, 583.

Kemp, Philip, & O'Keefe, Robert (2003). Improving teaching effectiveness. *College Teaching, 51*(3), 111-114. Retrieved August 11, 2007, from Wilson Education Abstracts database. (Document ID: 433579891).

Knowles, M., Holton, E., & Swanson, R. (2005). *The adult learner: The definitive classic in adult education and human resource development.* (6th ed.). Burlington, MA: Elsevier.

Kuhn T. (1996). *Structure of scientific revolutions* (3rd ed.). Chicago: University of Chicago Press.

Lavin, Angeline & Johnson, Stephen (2005). Preparation for the real business world: Empirical research in the MBA finance curriculum. College Student Journal, 39, 2, 377-401.

Layman, Lucas, Williams, Laurie, & Damian, Daniela (2006, September). Essential communication practices for eXtreme Programming in a global software development team. Information and Software Technology, 48, 9, 781.

LeProvost, J. & Mazur, G. (2005). Quality infrastructure improvement: using QFD to manage project priorities and project management resources. International Journal of Quality & Reliability Management, 22, 1, 10-16.

Lindstrom, Lowell & Jeffries, Ron (2004, Summer). eXtreme programming and agile software development methodologies. Information Systems Management, 21, 3, 41-60.

Long, Holly & Coldren, Jeffrey (2006). Interpersonal influences in large lecture-based classes: A socio-instructional perspective. *College Teaching, 54*(2), 237-243.

Retrieved August 11, 2007, from Wilson Education
Abstracts database. (Document ID: 1024088581).

Lord, Thomas, Shelly, Chad, & Zimmerman, Rachel (2007).
Putting inquiry teaching to the test: Enhancing learning
in college botany. *Journal of College Science
Teaching*, *36*(7), 62-65. Retrieved August 18, 2007,
from Wilson Education database. (Document
ID: 1296906551).

Lucas, Bill (2005, February). Mind your brain: why lifelong
learning matters: Part 2 What is lifelong
learning? *Training Journal*, 20-23. Retrieved August 31,
2007, from ABI/INFORM Global database. (Document
ID: 804298081).

Luftman, J. (2003). Assessing IT/Business Alignment.
Information Systems Management, 20, 9-15.

Margerison, Charles (2005, December). Great thinkers. *Training
Journal*,54. Retrieved August 31, 2007, from
ABI/INFORM Global database. (Document
ID: 1053627641).

Margulius, David L. (2005, December 5). Why IT needs strong
leaders. Info World, 27, 49, 22.

May, Thornton A. (2006, January 16). The time for leading is
upon us. Computerworld, 40, 3, 20-21.

McCall, Barry (2006). Breaking it down. *Business Review*, 11, 2,
4-5.

Meso, Peter & Jain, Radhika (2006). Agile software
development: adaptive systems principles and best
practices. Information Systems Management, 23(3), 19-
30.

Mingers, J. (2001), Combining IS research methods: Towards a pluralist methodology. Information Systems Research, 12, 3, 240-259.

Mir, Raza & Mir, Ali (2005, December). Catalysis, not leapfrog: An institutionalist argument for a limited role of ICTS in India's development. Asian Business and Management, 4, 4, 411.

Mojsilovi, A., Ray, B., Lawrence, R. & Takriti, S. (2007, December) A logistic regression framework for information technology outsourcing lifecycle management. Computers and Operations Research, 34, 12, 3609-3627.

Nord, Robert & Tomayko, James (2006, March/April). Software architecture-centric methods and agile development. IEEE Software, 23, 2, 47.

Notten, Ton (2002). Ambition and ambivalence, or: is there any system in andragology? *Systems Research and Behavioral Science, 19*(2), 137. Retrieved August 31, 2007, from ABI/INFORM Global database. (Document ID: 349161911).

Olague, Hector M., Etzkorn, Letha H., & Gholston, Sampson (2007, June). Empirical validation of three software metrics suites to predict fault-proneness of object-oriented classes developed using highly iterative or agile software development processes Transactions on Software Engineering, 33, 6; 402.

Palmer, P. (1998). *The courage to teach: Exploring the inner landscape of a teacher's life.* San Francisco: Jossey-Bass.

Pil, F. K. & Holweg, M. (2006). Evolving from value chain to value grid. MIT Sloan Management Review, 47, 4, 72-80.

Porter, M. (2001, March). Strategy and the internet. Harvard Business Review, 63-78.

RAYTHEON CO. V. HERNANDEZ (02-749) 540 U.S. 44 (2003). Legal Information Institute Website, Retrieved on July 20, 2012 from http://www.law.cornell.edu/supct/html/02-749.ZO.html

Rochester, Jack B. (1990, March). Improving application development productivity. I/S Analyzer, 28, 3, 1-12.

Romero, Tim (2002, December 11). The Black Team. *The Japan Times* (International), 7.6.

Sanchez-Rodriguez, Cristobal, Dewhurst, Frank, & Martinez-Lorente, Angel Rafael (2006). IT use in supporting TQM initiatives: an empirical investigation. International Journal of Operations and Production Management, 26, 5, 486.

Saran, Cliff (2007, March 20). Big changes come from small steps. Computer Weekly, 26.

Scandura, T. A. & Williams, E. A.(2000). Research methodology in management: Current practices, trends, and implications for future research. Academy of Management Journal, 43, 6, 1248-1264.

Scott, R. (2003). *Organizations: Rational, natural, and open systems* (5th ed.). Upper Saddle River, NJ: Prentice Hall.

Shenhar, Aaron, Milosevic, Dragan, Dvir, Dov, & Thamhain, Hans (2007, September). Linking project management to business strategy. PM Network, 21, 9, 91.

Shenk, K. D., Vitalari, N. P., & Davis, K. S. (1998). Differences between novice and expert systems analysts: What do we know and what do we do? *Journal of Management Information Systems*, 15, 9-50.

Song, Yong I. Rao, H. R., & Braynov , Sviatoslav B. (2004). Bringing E-government into the classroom: A case of e-commerce education. *Journal of Information Systems Education*, *15*(2), 127-137. Retrieved August 31, 2007, from ABI/INFORM Global database. (Document ID: 672480611).

Steenkamp, Annette Lerine & McCord, Samual Alan (2007, Summer). Approach to teaching research methodology for information technology. Journal of Information Systems Education, 2007, Summer, 18, 2, 255-262.

Sullivan, Laura (2004, July). The O word: Outsourcing overseas. Risk Management, 51, 7, 24-29.

Taylor, Hazel (2007, April - June). Outsourced IT projects from the vendor perspective: Different goals, different risks. Journal of Global Information Management, 15, 2, 1-21.

The U.S. Department of Labor Website (n.d.). Wage and hour division facts. Retrieved on August 18, 2012 from http://www.dol.gov/whd/regs/compliance/whdfs53.htm.

Tiwana, A.,Wang, J, Keil, M., and Ahluwalia, P. (2007, February). The bounded rationality bias in managerial valuation of real options: Theory and evidence from it projects. Decision Sciences, 38, 1, 157-181.

Torok, Sarah, McMorris, Robert, & Lin, Wen-Chi (2004). Is humor an appreciated teaching tool? Perceptions of professors' teaching styles and use of humor. *College Teaching*, 52(1), 14-20. Retrieved August 11, 2007, from Wilson Education database. (Document ID: 591062411).

Turk, Daniel, France, Robert, & Rumpe, Bernhard (2005,
October-December). Assumptions underlying agile
software development process. Journal of Database
Management, 16, 4, 62-87.

Van Rooij, Shahron (2007). Webmail versus webapp: Comparing
problem-based learning methods in a business research
methods course. Journal of Interactive Learning
Research, 18, 4, 555-569.

Vella, J., Berardinelli, P., & Burrow, J. (1998). *How do they know
they know: Evaluating adult learning*. San Francisco:
Jossey-Bass Publishers.

Willcocks, L.P. and Lester, S. (1997). In search of information
technology productivity: assessment issues. Journal of
the Operational Research Society, 48, 11, 1082-1094.

Williams, Kathy (2006, January). Professional accountants in
business are valuable. Strategic Finance, 87, 7, 23.

Yu, Huiming, Wang, Linsong, Zhang, Jing, Barksdale, Jeremy, &
Yuan, Xiaohong (2006). Developing a secure geospatial
visualization and collaboration system using software
engineering technology. International Journal of
Computers and Applications, 28, 4, 350-358.

Zadrozny, M. A. & Ferrazzi, K. E. (1992, Fall). Building a
technology basis for TQM. Chief Information Officer
Journal, 16-20.

Zemke, R. (2001, June). Learning as Conversation. *Training*, 14.

Zin, Abdullah Mohd, Idris, Sufian, & Subramamian, Nantha
Kumar (2006, Summer). Journal of Information Systems
Education, 17, 2, 113-117.